Using Your Turn Signal Promotes World Peace

More Observations from a Working Poet

Poets notice what other people miss.
Nationally-known poet Molly Fisk's singular
perspective on love, death, grammar, lingerie,
small towns, and the natural world
will get you laughing, crying, and thinking.

Using Your Turn Signal Promotes World Peace

More Observations from a Working Poet

Molly Fisk

Story Street Press
Nevada City, California
2015

Published by Story Street Press
10068 Newtown Rd.
Nevada City, CA 95959
e-mail: molly@mollyfisk.com
www.mollyfisk.com

This edition was produced for on-demand distribution by
ingramspark.com and createspace.com for Story Street Press.

Cover design: Maxima Kahn
Cover photo ('53 Chevy half-ton pick-up only): Peter Fisk
Author photo: Justin Bailey
Typesetting: Wordsworth (wordsworthofmarin.com)
Moral Support: Julia Kelliher, Joanna Robinson, Nancy Shanteau
Technical Support: Paul Emery, Steve Baker, Bren Smith,
Jeffrey & Shawna Hein
Marketing Support: Susanna Wilson, Maxima Kahn, Sarah
Griscom, Heidi LeVell, Andrew Hoerner, Jenny Shih, Anna
Kunneke, Pamela Biery
Original inspiration: Carolyn Crane
Contributing Caffienation: Sierra Mountain Coffee Roasters
Frequency: KVMR 89.5 FM Nevada City, CA (105.1 Truckee,
104.7 Woodland, 88.3 Placerville, kvmr.org), The California
Report, KQED 88.5 FM San Francisco, CA (89.3 Sacramento)

Printed in the United States of America

978-0-9894958-2-0

Dedicated to the brave and patient four
who taught me to drive:

Antoinette (Toni) Entwistle Pennington Fisk
Irving Lester Fisk, II
Erma Johnson (Jonnie) Fisk
Margaret Anne (Peggy) Thurston

and everyone, everywhere, who works toward peace.

Also by Molly Fisk

Blow-Drying a Chicken (radio commentary, 2013)

The More Difficult Beauty (poetry, 2010)

"Blow-Drying a Chicken" (CD, 2008)

"Using Your Turn Signal Promotes World Peace"
(limited edition CD, 2005)

Listening to Winter (poetry, 2000)

Terrain (poetry, with Dan Bellm & Forrest Hamer,
1998)

"Surrender" (limited edition audio tape, 1994)

Salt Water Poems (poetry, limited edition letterpress,
Jungle Garden Press, 1994)

Contents

YIELD

ONE WAY

U-TURNS

LEFT TURNS

Google

This week I'm finding it very hard not to be a language snob. I don't want to be a language snob, or any kind of snob. I want to be one of the people, progressive and open-hearted, equal to everyone else, with liberty and justice for all. But then some chowder-head uses the word Google as a verb and all my best intentions disintegrate.

Google is not a verb. Google is a brand name, like Kleenex and Tampax and Electro-Lux. Bad enough that brand names sneak into our brains to usurp the rightful places of actual nouns, like tissue or tampon or vacuum cleaner. Now they're trying to become verbs.

Think of the horrible precedent this sets! If you can Google a fact or question, then it stands to reason you can Kleenex your nose when you're about to sneeze, or call out to your wife when she gets home from work, "Just a minute, honey, I'm

Electro-Luxing the guest room!" Pretty soon we'll be Nissaning down to the grocery store and Tiding our clothes when they're dirty, Maybellining our eyelashes, and Arcoing our cars whenever the tank gets low. The English language will go straight down the drain.

You can stop this, you know you can. It just takes a tiny effort. Repeat after me: *I'm going to look that up on Google, check Google for the answer, see if I can find it on Google. I'll visit Google, click on Google, ask the good folks at Google. If any place will have it, it's got to be Google.*

Maybe we can't save the world from flood and pestilence, but we can save our language from being taken over by the corporate advertising machine. I have no quarrel with the search engine Google, I think it's enormously useful. It just needs to be kept in its proper place and not allowed to run roughshod over the common vocabulary.

We lost this fight with Xerox long ago, and more recently with Fed Ex. *Don't worry, I'll Xerox the contract and Fed Ex it to you* is etched in the professional vernacular, and many of us running small businesses get caught up in it, too, although personally I try to say "copy" and "ship," instead. I realize most Americans do the easy thing and wrap their tongues around those seductive Xs. Go ahead, if you really want to give these companies free advertising.

I know the English language is always in flux, that words come and go, that Shakespeare invented "bump" and J. M. Barrie made up the name "Wendy" to go with Peter Pan, and both are still with us. I know that "queer" and "gay" and "fairy" have taken on new meaning in the last half-century. I'm not opposed to this — change is a sign of life. I just hate to see *commerce* get any more of its hooks into us.

Which is why, when I hear someone say he's going to go Google something, my upper lip lifts in an almost imperceptible sneer and I think to myself: *Oh, good grief. What a Yahoo.*

Watch Your Language

By this time in your lives, I'm sure you've all
heard that Eskimos have 68 words for snow, or 409
or something. I don't know where this idea came
from, but whenever I talk to anyone about language
and how it represents culture, they nod sagely and
tell me that the Eskimos have so-and-so-many words
for snow. It's never the same number. And it's never
that the Aborigines have X number of words for
horizon, or the Tahitians have Y number for sand.
Somehow Eskimos became the example — probably
in a 4th grade textbook that was distributed to all
U.S. public schools in 1956.

This week a friend who knows I've been to
Lapland sent me an article. The story is that
because of global warming, migratory birds are
inching their way farther north every year, causing
confusion to populations who've never seen them

before. So the Lapps, who according to this article have 1200 words for reindeer, don't have any words for barn owl or robin or titmouse.

Well, I live smack in the middle of titmouse territory, and I still only have one word for them. But I do have several words for woodpecker. Around here we have Ladderback, Red-headed, and Nuttall's woodpeckers, although it took me a long time to figure out that the ones nesting in my apple tree were Nuttall's, because they look quite unlike any of the pictures in Peterson or Sibley.

I can imagine inventing a new word for my particular woodpeckers, along the lines of Nuttall-with-no-red-neck-patch, or something. I assume that's how all those reindeer names were invented, through trying to identify specific variations: cantankerous old reindeer with broken antler, pregnant reindeer who always drops twins and they live.

No one goes to this kind of trouble unless it's important to them. If people in my town were trying to make a living off of titmice, you know we'd have more words for them. Instead, I'm sorry to say, what we have a lot of words for are complicated coffee drinks. Also cars. Things we have around us in large number and need to be able to identify. I find this enormously depressing, but keep in mind that I didn't choose to stay in Lapland, I was only there for three weeks and it was summer.

The corollary to this language-as-culture idea came from one of my students, who brought in a poem the other day called "Amrita." When we looked blank, she said it was an ancient word, probably Sanskrit, for the mixing of sexual juices. One delicate word for something that it takes a lot of fumbling and blushing to say in five words of English.

Language is a big mirror. It reflects back to us what we as a group are interested in. I hope you're thinking what I'm thinking. Time to brush up on our Sanskrit. And learning a language is so much easier with a partner...

Getting Into Mischief

My wonderful niece Gioia is coming to town this weekend with her mom. We're planning to flail around on cross country skis for a while, eat sushi for dinner, and at some point Gioia will give me this look, this arched-eye-browed, slightly challenging look that everyone says she learned from me, and say, "When are we going to get into some mischief?"

This is totally my own fault. Gioia is almost nine, and ever since she was five I've been doing my best to subvert the essential goodness and propriety taught her by her parents. They're not straight-laced or strict or anything, unless you think a Waldorf education is strict. They're just good — naturally good — and I, for all my wonderful qualities, am not really all that good. I've been working for the last 20 years on throwing goodness out the window and trying to be myself instead, concentrating hard on irreverence and humor.

The first thing I taught Gioia to do was put canned goods inside all her father's shoes. She'd sneak into the guest bed with me early in the morning and we'd wait for him to get dressed and let out a loud squawk when his foot found the cold round surface of a can of refried beans. After that she graduated to exchanging her parents' dresser drawers — her mother's lingerie we'd move down to where the sweaters lived, put the sweaters where the pants had been, and stuff the jeans and cords into the lingerie drawer. You'd be surprised at how much pleasure this brings a child. And, of course, a lot of the fun is waiting to be found out. Luckily her parents played the game well, squealing and hollering in mock outrage, and weren't too irritated with me. I think they secretly appreciated a short vacation from goodness themselves.

When you don't have your own children, you aren't accustomed to having to deal with the consequences of what you've started, since you — I should say I — sweep in, cause a bunch of trouble, and then go home to sit peacefully in front of the fire and read a book. Meanwhile Gioia has to be calmed down from the heights of her glee so she can be put to bed, and a lot of clothing and canned food needs to be relocated.

It turns out, however, that I may have painted myself into a corner. As Gioia's getting older, her ideas of mischief are becoming more inventive. She's picked up some of that irreverence and rebellion I wanted her to learn. And although her innate good nature is very strong and she would never want to hurt anyone, I worry that she'll think of something potentially really irritating, like hiding car keys in the freezer or painting somebody's windshield with peanut butter. Then everyone will blame me, and rightly so.

My brother is of course delighted that I have to suffer too, watching me think fast on my feet to keep one step ahead of his smart daughter.

Wait till I teach her to short-sheet his bed.

Procrastinating

For the last three weeks I've been preparing a new talk. Well, let me rephrase that: for the last three weeks I've been *saying* I was preparing a new talk and getting *ready* to start working on the talk but mostly balancing my bank statement and doing a lot of mending that's been sitting in a pile for six months but suddenly seems incredibly urgent.

I hate to admit it, but despite turning all my papers in on time in college, I am an ace procrastinator. I've fought this notion for years, because we all know that procrastinating is morally suspect and liable to undermine the fabric of society. First I rigidly refused to procrastinate and instead wasted lots of time working very slowly and steadily and meeting the deadline. While this looks like the proper way to accomplish things, it felt like an enormous burden. Then I secretly sneered at other procrastinators, arguing inside my head that my tendency to "do things at the last minute" was a creative maneuver, not just sloth or poor time management like theirs was.

Luckily for my character development, I eventually realized that my procrastinating was exactly like everyone else's and this secret sneering business was going to undermine my moral fibers a lot faster than the procrastination itself. I decided to look at the way I did things, and see what was going on. I wanted to know whether procrastinating was a true drawback, or if it might actually serve some function for me.

When I have a project or deadline of some sort, at first my brain says, "Oh, there's plenty of time, don't worry about that yet." I talk to my friends about whatever the subject is and randomly look for reference materials, but I don't concentrate very hard. At a certain point in the time-line, my brain switches over to: "OK, it really is time to work on that, but let's just do this one thing first." Even when I'm mending curtains that my cats have ripped off the wall, part of my mind is mulling the project over.

Then comes a crucial moment, four to six days before the deadline, when suddenly I leap into action — thinking, writing, getting everything organized — and I feel incredibly alive. The right proportion of pent-up energy has finally been let loose, and I think I'm smarter and better at making mental connections because of it. And the whole thing is easier and more fun than it was when I started earlier and paced myself.

The only delicate part of the process is if I wait too long to spring into action, because then panic sets in. The thought that I'll screw up because I'm unprepared overwhelms my ability to think clearly about the project itself. Unfortunately, I think that's where I am now. I'm a poet, I don't know how to give a talk — what will I say?

This question makes my friends — rat finks that they are — break into hysterics. "YOU? Molly Fisk? Not have something to *say*?!!!"

Lie Down

Look, can we just get one thing straight? When
you're talking about amounts of something, you use
"less" with stuff that can't be individually counted,
and "fewer" with what can — less water, fewer
leaks...less money, fewer dollars...less fun, fewer
laughs. Got it?

While we're on the subject of language, let me
tell you that the way to make the opposite sex, or
the same sex if that's your fancy, turn their heads
is to use more interesting verbs. I swear, this
technique is better than a Wonderbra, or that sleek
black Lamborghini you can't afford. Those will work
on some people, but do you really want to drive too
fast with a person who just likes you for your car?
And after you've laid that lingerie across the back
of his sofa, what will you say next? *Come here, baby*
is a little tame, not to mention overused. *Slide your
sweet self over here* is better, or *Slither into my arms,*

darling, so I can slather you with kisses. Trust me, it's the verbs.

Which brings me to the huge problem of "lay." I really don't know what happened to this poor verb, but it's taken more of a beating than any other. Maybe it's the old prayer: "Now I lay me down to sleep." People got confused and shortened it to "Now I lay down" and the whole conjugation fell apart. It's LIE down. You only lay, in the present tense, when you're placing something — it's a synonym for "put."

Now, bear with me. Here they are in a sentence: "Mom, I feel kind of funky, I'm going to lay down." Or, conversely, "Wyatt Earp, lay down your guns or I'll shoot you full of holes!" Try substituting "put" in those two sentences: "Mom, I'm going to put down" doesn't work at all — put down what? But "put down your guns" makes perfect sense. Things get dicier, of course, when we add the past tense to this discussion, because the past tense for *lie* is lay, which totally confuses everyone.

Who cares about this stuff? A whole bunch of us do — we hate, despise, regret, and deplore the bedraggled state of the English language. But I'm not perfect, either. I make a lot of mistakes, usually with split infinitives. It just depends on how your ear was trained. I wince when someone says "less chances," but I can't even think of an example to give you of how not to split an infinitive. Just do the best you can.

And remember, if you want to get laid by anyone with half a brain, lay your inhibitions to one side, lie down somewhere comfortable, and murmur your most exciting and lascivious verbs.

Salvage Yard Windows

When I was rebuilding my house, seven years ago, I spent a lot of time at salvage yards. I found a good porcelain tub with no nicks and bought the claw feet separately. I found a lovely front door, which now has vines and pears and apples and birds painted all over it. I completely lucked out with a medicine chest, beveled mirror intact, for five bucks. But these were small potatoes. My real find was the windows.

I like the dark, especially at night, especially outdoors. It doesn't scare me — it's kind of comforting. But indoors I want as much natural light as I can get. Unlike most of my ex-boyfriends, who preferred their curtains drawn, I want sun streaming in and lifting my mood, which can tend to the morose if I'm not careful.

So I wanted lots of windows in the new house but new windows, as you know, aren't cheap. I

borrowed a friend's truck and went exploring. In
Sacramento there were two salvage places in the
same block of 16th St. One was kind of upscale: a
big warehouse full of clean windows and doors. After
a few afternoons there I bought three long narrow
windows, divided by mullions into four panes each.
One was smaller than the others. We put it next to
the front door, vertically, with hinges so it would
open. The other two we framed into the corner of
the living room, very close together, where they
overlook the old apple tree's massive trunk.

The other salvage yard was one of those places
with broken glass and piles of rusting grocery carts
and machinery you can't identify. It had some great
hanging lamps, the kind you'd put low over a pool
table, but I didn't have room for a pool table. There
were probably five thousand windows standing
helter-skelter under a tin awning outside. I'm quite
sure there were rats living in this chaos, but I went
back week after week, trying to find what I needed
and coming home frustrated and empty-handed.

Finally Rodger, my house builder, said, *I need
the windows tomorrow*. Groaning, I drove down
there again, tape measure in hand. After three
hours, I'd found eight half-windows, the sash kind,
of the right dimension. They weren't identical: half

were six-paned and half had no mullions at all, but they had to do. After some head-scratching, Rodger and I configured them so they abutted the corner windows, the plain glass ones first, and then the six-over-sixes, and made a lovely bank of light across two living room walls.

This completely transformed the house. In summer, the apple's leaves block out the road and give me some privacy: it's like being in a tree house, only more comfortable. Finches and titmice race around in the branches.

Spring's the best, though. When the apple tree blooms and all you can see is pink and white and all you can hear is the fizz of bees, it's like living inside a bouquet, or a poem.

89 Chairs

I'm not sure what's happening, but some
natural, organic process — maybe aging? maybe
just living — is insisting that I simplify my life.
A little voice in my head wants the same food for
breakfast every day. My eyes feel tired of looking at
all the stuff in my house: my great-grandmother's
tea cups, seashells I found in Key West displayed
on a little wooden shelf bracket from Norway.
The big drawer of loose photographs I never seem
to deal with. Cast iron, mixing bowls, too many
t-shirts.

I'm not a true hoarder, because I purge things
every couple of years, and you can always walk
unimpeded through my house. But there's a lot of
accumulation around me right now, and it's driving
me "bat guano crazy." How many soup bowls does
one woman need? I do not have house parties where
luncheon for 12 is on the schedule.

The last object I went nuts for was a ceramic creamer from Heath Ceramics in Sausalito. Anyone growing up near San Francisco in the 1960s, whose parents were of a certain class and aesthetic bent, ate their meals off Heath stoneware, including me. The shapes of the design are both classic and iconic, and to my eye that mix of beautiful and familiar is pretty irresistible. I cajoled my sister into giving me this pitcher for Christmas last year. When was the last time I served anybody cream in my kitchen? Maybe a decade ago. I filled it with maple syrup once for a breakfast gathering, and sometimes I'll plunk a few flowers in it from the yard, but most of the time it sits in a cabinet out of sight.

The 19th century British architect and textile designer William Morris famously said "Have nothing in your house that you do not know to be useful or believe to be beautiful." I love this quote, but I think he might have added that no one needs more than one of each of these things... There's so much stuff on the planet already, most of it in the houses of first world residents like me, that it's crazy, and they're making more of everything in China as we speak, which is even crazier.

This weekend I'm going to pack up a few boxes and take them to the thrift store. Kids these days are ingeniously recycling and up-cycling, which is a wonderful thing. I'm sure someone out there will love drinking tea from my great-grandmother's cups, or perhaps making them into wind chimes.

E.B. White, the author of *Charlotte's Web*, lived for many years in New York City. He finally moved permanently to his summer house in Maine when he realized that between both houses, he and his wife owned 89 chairs.

That's a good bellwether for excess. How many chairs do you own? This morning's count at my house was 14 inside and 16 out on my decks. 30 chairs. I live alone. Does this make *any* sense? No, I didn't think so.

My Bear

I've been feeling kind of irritable lately —
uncomfortable in my own skin and cantankerous
about it. Things that never used to bother me —
like middled-aged men in green Subarus who pass
a parking spot at the market and then change
their minds, backing up to take it, and motioning
me to back up so they can angle in when I was
going to park there myself — make me furious.
I was actually ready to slap one such person
the other day, but by the time I parked he had
disappeared into the store.

I should have gone home right then, because
my errand was useless. I managed to purchase
the wrong sized track light bulb, triple A batteries
instead of double A — prudently buying the
economy size — and sourdough bread rather
than multi-grain. When I unpacked the bag in my
kitchen, all I could do was laugh, and wonder at

the power of anger to addle my usually well-oiled
brain. I have sometimes bought the wrong battery
by misremembering what I needed, but never before
have I looked at three A's and seen only two.

One moral of this story is never tailgate green
Subarus in grocery store parking lots. Another
moral is that learning to laugh at your own mistakes
will save you. It's only taken me 50 years to figure
this out, but what's half a century of effort when the
results are so useful?

And there's something I haven't told you yet.
I think the reason I'm feeling so disgruntled these
days is that I was hexed by a bear.

Where I live, bears are not that common.
Newspaper stories describe what pests they are
getting into peoples' trash up at Lake Tahoe, or
how one's been spotted ambling across a highway,
stopping traffic. This bear — *my* bear — was racing
pell-mell through the trees on a rainy night about
nine o'clock, and jumped off a high bank into
Empress Road just as I had turned the corner and
gotten to the same spot on the asphalt. Luckily
there was room for both of us, and we moved
forward together at breakneck speed for a few
moments. My heart was in my throat, my voice
uttered the same stupid swear word over and over.

Then I remembered that bears can get into locked cars — they do it in Yosemite, easy as opening a tuna can — so I sped up and left the bear behind.

Because it felt as if the bear was jumping off the bank onto my left shoulder, and because her back was as tall as the hood of my car, I drove perhaps further than was strictly necessary before curiosity kicked in. Then I went back, but she was gone. No crashing through the underbrush, no gleaming yellow eyes. Maybe it was the adrenaline coursing through my veins, but I was wildly disappointed. I hadn't been able to look at her long enough — my impression was only of hugeness, and very large feet. She was a dark color, but was it brown or black? Was she sleek? I never found out.

It took me forever to get to sleep that night, but ever since I seem to sleep more and more. And this surliness has come over me, accompanied by sudden desires to slap people. I'm pretty sure that bear worked some kind of magic on me. Reading the paper this morning, I caught myself gnashing my teeth.

We, the People

The phone rang early this morning and though I
looked up, I didn't answer it. I love Al Gore, I loved
his movie, and I agree with many of his political
opinions — I even think he's sexier now that he's
put on a little weight. I just don't want to hear his
prerecorded voice at 7 a.m.

Luckily, it wasn't Al, it was Kate. I love Kate
too, and agree with many of *her* opinions. Since she
doesn't tape her message, she can call any time.
Thirty years from now, when I'm either moldering
in my grave or sashaying through Venezuela
with Elder Hostel, no one will think twice about
talking to computers on the phone. Phones will be
implanted in our heads by then, and the computers
will be outsourced to Mars. But today, I find the
whole idea revolting.

I knew I was going to turn into a curmudgeon,
I just didn't think it would happen this soon. I well

remember the look of horror on my grandmother's face as someone at a neighboring restaurant table applied her lipstick in public. Adhering to that kind of standard seems ludicrous today, when we've been so inured, through movie sex and just walking around town, to the public display of body parts. No one much turns a hair when people start changing their clothes at the next table. But at the time, it was scandalous.

Now I know exactly how my grandmother felt. I'm not a universal curmudgeon. New gadgets — DVD players and Blue Tooth, whatever that is — don't automatically cheer me up, but they don't offend me, either. What raises my blood pressure is invasion of privacy, and the new ways people find to be impersonal.

Our culture presents us with an obscene number of options for every possible product or service. You can't walk two blocks without getting bombarded with ads. Now they aren't even waiting for us to choose, they're phoning to remind us which choice they want us to go for.

My house is a private place, and I want it to stay that way. I turn on the radio and TV only when I feel like it. I answer the door if it's a neighbor's kid, and not when I see members of proselytizing

religions pull into the driveway. I'm in charge here.
If you want to talk to me, I don't care if you're the
King of Siam, you can damn well call me in person.

The irony is, it would be a better political move.
If Al Gore actually did call some of us in person,
we'd tell everyone we know within hours. They'd
tell their friends, and it would spread like a grass
fire. He'd reach many more of us, and we'd be
better disposed to listen to his message because he
treated us like human beings instead of potential
consumers. The powers that be seem to forget we're
real people, as in that line no one remembers any
more.

You know, the one that starts out: "We the
People."

Candlelight

I went to a candlelight vigil last week in support of Domestic Violence Prevention Month. We were honoring both the idea of ending this kind of violence, and a specific tragedy: a woman in our town was recently murdered in her home. I didn't know her. Before she was killed, I had never heard her name. But this being a small town, I knew the social worker who was on duty at the hospital the day she died, the one who talked to her friends and devastated family for hours. And I knew the sister of a friend of the woman's brother, who picked him up at the airport when he arrived to face the aftermath of this terrible situation.

I knew hardly anyone at the vigil, which surprised me. Last spring I spoke at a vigil in support of Child Abuse Prevention Month, and I knew hardly anyone there, either. On any given night around here, you

can probably choose between ten important and
interesting things to do. Still, I was a little startled
to be in a crowd of strangers, and I was sad that my
closest friends weren't with me.

Given my own experience with domestic
violence, I'm not that comfortable mingling with
people I don't know in the dark, and several times I
thought of leaving. What kept me there weren't the
testimonials given over a scratchy sound system, nor
the earnest but unintelligible middle school choir.
What held my attention, unexpectedly, was beauty.

I hope some time you'll get a chance to see 200
candles stretched over three city blocks. The faces
of the people who carried them were lit from below,
haloed in reverse. We walked slowly up a small
hill, around a corner through town, past closed
store-fronts, open bars, the movie theater's bright
marquee, and back down a side street that wasn't
well-lit, skirting a municipal parking lot. Once we
got past the ambient light, we looked like pilgrims
walking the Camino in Spain, or believers at the
Wailing Wall in Jerusalem.

We looked like what we were. Just humans. A
temporary community. In our sweaters and jackets,
our blue hair, plaid shirts, and wool scarves, our
pierced tongues and work boots. Old and young.

Female and male. We looked like hope and sorrow and thoughtfulness and confusion. Like despair. Like companionship. Like resignation. Forgiveness right next to unforgiving.

People walked arm in arm or single file. Some talked and some were silent. Some wept. Some laughed. The local cops looked after us when we overflowed the sidewalks and spilled into the street. Many moms had brought their daughters. There were grown men there, and teenaged boys. Lots of girls and women. Little kids playing tag and shrieking.

And one sweet three-year-old who held her mother's hand the whole way and never stopped singing.

RIGHT TURNS

What I Love

Today, here's what I love: the sight of a cat's
front half under the rug and his stillness, his
completely mistaken conviction that no one can see
him. The fact that my arms are still strong enough
to carry eight pieces of stove wood at a time. The
way that buck outside eating the new growth off
my Photinia flips his big oven-mitt of an ear from
behind his antler to the front, grazing the horn a
little — casually alert.

I love radio for its disembodied company as I
wash the dishes, and I love apple-scented dish soap.
I love the mottled bowls my cousin Rapp turned
and glazed and fired and gave me in trade for a
Norwegian sweater I knit him in 1982. The way
their round sides gleam in the drainer as the sun
inches up over Cement Hill, slips past the neon sign
at the Willo, and blazes into my kitchen windows all
at once, like a wave breaking.

Somebody said that love is a verb — a statement nearly moronic in its obviousness if you're looking at it grammatically. The point being that in order to have love in your life you have to start loving, rather than wait for love, the noun, to be handed to you. Wading bravely through my distaste for psychological platitudes, I do understand this, although I think the phrase was coined in reference specifically to romantic love. Romance is great, don't get me wrong, but proportionately it makes up only a small part of a life. Love, on the other hand, is huge, and as necessary to our individual days as breathing.

What is it, anyway? Probably, everyone has their own definition, this being a free country. Mine is gladness, surprise, delight, a deep attention; sometimes a feeling of unmarred connection; benevolent and abiding support for something inside or outside ourselves. Depending on a host of factors, love can fall from your lips as easy as song or stick in your throat, unspoken.

It makes sense to me to practice love, to acknowledge it out loud, in the same way that people work their muscles through exercise, or flex their brains by reading and thinking. Love as a practice feels similar to daily prayer or meditation,

as a way to keep the channels to whatever is out
there open. As with hiking, yoga, or crosswords,
start slowly — you don't want to sprain your heart.
Find one thing to love today and praise it.

I love writing. I love the words *benevolent* and
platitude, how they sound in my mouth, the click
of the Ts falling into place like dominoes. I love
that cliché "to coin a phrase." Can't you just see its
making? Hot silver being poured oh-so-carefully into
the little mold — enough to pick out every detail,
not so much that it overflows. A quick dip into ice
water, the hiss and steam, and a shiny new phrase
rolls onto the table — bright, untarnished — ready
for someone like you or me to give it our surprise
and delight, our vast, best, down-home, fearless,
complete, and uncomplicated love.

Rag Dolls

When I was 12, I started my first business:
selling rag dolls. I did not invent these, they were
cut from a Mary Poppins doll-making kit that my
mother gave me for Christmas when I was ten. That
year I made one doll. Mom helped me turn the fabric
arms and legs right-side-out after I'd stitched them,
and provided the cast-off nylon stockings I used for
stuffing, but otherwise I did it all by myself and was
pretty darn smug.

The doll did not look like Julie Andrews,
thank heavens — more like a cross between Laura
Ingalls Wilder and Frida Kahlo. The Frida aspect
was due to my following the instructions, which
said after embroidering one eyebrow on the face
fabric, you could run the thread behind the fabric
to do the other eyebrow instead of knotting and
cutting it and starting fresh. I don't think the kit's
designers had tried this with white skin fabric and

black eyebrow embroidery floss. When the doll was finished, the line of thread between the eyebrows was quite visible. This did not interrupt my pride of accomplishment for very long, however. My mother — who smocked our dresses and knit us all Xmas stockings with fuzzy yarn for Santa's beard — was pretty thrilled too.

I have no memory of the moment I thought of selling the dolls. Maybe a comment from one of my parents' friends was the spark. I also have no memory of going to the stores. I'm sure I took five or six dolls with me — all in different-colored dresses, with red or yellow or brown or black yarn for hair — and I'm sure I was terrified. I was paid an incredible $10 for each one, and everybody wanted more.

Before you wince at the price, $10 in 1967 is about $70 today. Now you can wince. That was a wage of approximately 40 cents an hour. Since I was 12 and our family didn't lack for money, hourly rates meant nothing to me. I was just amazed that something I made could sell in a store.

I sewed 27 rag dolls before I burned out on the tiny hand-stitched lace hems and black felt high-button boots and had to go to high school. But the entrepreneurial itch has never left me. For ten years I designed Norwegian-style sweaters and sold them to swank boutiques on the East Coast, substituting pterodactyls or seahorses for the expected reindeer. Now my prestidigious fingers have turned from stitching to typing and I teach poetry classes over the Internet. I love the work, but I miss that glorious sense of wealth when I'd look at the seven dolls or 35 sweaters covering my kitchen table. Tangible things I made myself: clean and perfect and in multiples! There's nothing like it.

I had forgotten the feeling entirely until yesterday, when UPS brought two enormous boxes to my front door, filled with copies of my new CD of radio essays. Suddenly I was 12 again, gazing at what I made with my own two hands. What abundance! What a *harvest*.

Sandhill Cranes & Gary Snyder

One thing I like about this town is how many other writers live here. Sometimes I see them in coffee shops or over breakfast at Ike's or South Pine. At a concert two or three of us will say hello, and certainly if anyone's published a book, a bunch of us will show up at the reading. There's a particular smile and sometimes a little shrug that writers will give each other, a kind of expression that says "I know you. I know what it's like, and I'm doing it too, and isn't it great, or hard, or nuts that we spend our lives this way?" We know we're part of the same tribe, whether poets or novelists or writers of kid's books or creative non-fiction. Even journalists, who have a different pace to their days, are part of the gang.

I don't socialize that much with other writers — we don't have all-writer dinner parties or anything. I don't necessarily know what people are working on, or what classes they might have started teaching. I don't need to be in constant touch with them — in fact, that would probably be a burden. What I like is knowing that when I'm sitting at my desk, putting in a comma, changing it to a dash, and then taking it out again, a few other people out there are doing it too. They understand how necessary it is, even though the rest of the world is mystified.

That sense of invisible camaraderie is really useful during those times we lose our perspective, when we think, as I was just thinking this morning, that we're washed up, has-beens, that we'll never write as well again as our last book or poem.

I hate this part of the job, but it seems to happen to everyone: those hours or days or months when you think you're just awful at writing, you should quit and go work on a CalTrans crew, everyone else is better than you are and they're certainly winning more prizes, have better agents, get bigger advances. They're definitely happier. Writing comes *easily* to them.

Once in a while this stage of the writing life lasts extra-long and seems impossible to break out of. That's pretty much where I am now. Demoralized, despondent, despairing, and really bored with myself. Writing poem after dreadful poem and wondering why I bother.

But today, for a little while, I got saved. From my desk I heard — very faintly, but unmistakeable — a swooping, heart-stopping sound. I raced outside, and looked up. At first I couldn't see them in the clouds, and then I did — their loose vees forming and dissolving high in the sky, almost invisible. About a hundred of them, black ribbons against the gray. I knew what they were because Gary Snyder told me once that he watched for them every spring. They were heading his way on their long trip to Montana or Saskatchewan, but passed over my place first, a random blessing.

Sandhill cranes, migrating north. A gift from another writer. A reminder to love the world.

A Poet's Day

This morning I taught 6th graders to
write poetry using a technique called surreal
juxtaposition, which I explain to them just means
putting weird things next to each other. We played
a game that resulted in phrases like: *the frozen
armchair of bent jurisprudence*, and *whirling
skateboards of desperate self-discipline*. That took 42
minutes. Then I bought gas and a cup of coffee and
went to a friend's house to get a few more details
from her in order to write her son's obituary. This
was our second day talking about him, so I was only
there for an hour and a half, and only twice did I
burst into tears.

I came home, answered three phone calls and
eight e-mails, and typed up my notes, trying not
to forget anything she told me and to make the
paragraphs and quotations sound as though they
belonged to each other. I wove in the thoughts

this boy's dad had e-mailed to me as well, read the
whole thing to my friend over the phone, made
some corrections, printed it out, and delivered it
to *The Union* so it would make tomorrow's paper.
All of that took about three hours, well, four if you
count drive time, buying another cup of coffee and
an egg-salad sandwich, and preventing several cats
from sitting on the keyboard. I also spent a couple of
minutes not looking at the huge pile of laundry on
my bedroom floor and the revolting conditions in the
bathroom.

Then I brought a copy of the obituary back to
my friend's house, gave her a quick hug and hopped
in the car again to drive to the hospital, where I
teach writing to cancer patients. Now I'm sitting at
a long formica table, watching my students (some
with their own hair, some with wigs or hats on) do
a 15-minute free write on who their heroes are.
I've already had them do warm-ups: writing about
water, fire, their favorite shoes, and where their
grandfathers came from. Today, I love these people
more fiercely than usual, which I guess is where
writing obituaries will get you.

At the end of this two-hour class I'll go home
and feed the cats, water the parched and gasping
yard, and probably eat two tomatoes out of my hand

for dinner. There isn't anything else palatable in the house that I know of, except ice cubes. I may or may not manage to stay awake until 8:30.

Why am I telling you this? People are so mystified by what a poet does all day. This isn't a typical day, of course, it's more packed with fresh grief than usual, includes a little more driving. But it's in the ballpark. Just so you'll understand when you next walk up to me on the street and say "Have you written any poems lately?" and I smile and say, "No, not lately."

F.I.N.E., Fine

I'm a little startled to mention this, but you
know what? Everything is alright in my little home-
made life, which has sometimes looked like the
aftermath of Chernobyl. There isn't even a leaky
faucet. No cat barf on the rug. Nobody's ill, no one is
sad. We're in bright immediate Spring, so no plants
are dying of thirst yet. The lawn is mowed, the shed
is clean, and the scrap metal guys came yesterday to
take away the bent garage door that's been driving
me crazy. Everything is hunky-dory, from the bees in
the apple blossoms to the bluebirds nesting in their
box just outside the cat fence.

I see two small miracles here. One is: I can say
this and not be a size 6, or even a 12. Used to was,
my weight defined the household mood. At some
point when I wasn't looking, that changed. I'm still
"larger than the average bear," as Yogi used to say,
and that can be irritating, but it's not central. What's

central is a kind of amiable low-grade enjoyment of
the world. I get sharp pangs of joy at — for instance
— a lunar eclipse, but there's a lot of moderate glee
underneath that, for ordinary beauty like blue-bellied
lizards and spiderwebs covered with dew.

The other miracle is how much I've learned
to appreciate what I have. I don't want to sound
prissy or self-congratulatory, like one more awful
righteous meme scrolling through your Facebook
news feed. I'm not quoting Eckhart, Marianne, or
even David Whyte. This came upon me unawares,
after years of learning about unconscious privilege
from my friends who aren't white and weren't
raised upper-middle class. Instead of looking at what
I lacked: children, a man who adores me, a famous
publisher for my books, I began to see how much
good I'd been given for no reason. Health, smarts,
red hair, thousands of opportunities I blithely took
for granted. Sure, I work hard and try to do my
best most of the time, but lucky breaks, cultural
privilege, my own expectations, and a genetically-
infectious grin have carried me a long way, too.
These things aren't fair, but they're real, and
recognizing that realness has given me a breadth of
gratitude I never had before. Feeling guilty about
something you can't control is kind of useless, so

now I work on equalizing unfairness in the world
without that straight-jacket of guilt.

When I was in 12-Step programs a few decades
ago, we used to joke about the word "fine."

"How are you?" We'd ask each other.

"Oh, fine!" someone would respond.

For us, "fine" was an acronym for Fucked
up, Insecure, Neurotic, and Exhausted, an apt
description of how it feels to recover from addiction.

Today, over at my house, five out of five cats
agree that it just means "fine." AOK, copasetic,
peachy keen, no disasters.

Plain and simple. Nothing ironic about it.

Very Famous

This week I have been *very* famous. My new
website went live after three months of work,
my CD of essays came out, and there was a fairly
revealing article about me in our local newspaper.

All this notoriety led my bank manager to throw
herself into my arms and give me a huge hug —
ditto from a local realtor whom I know only by sight.
The women I work out with teased me about my
fancy education, and wouldn't let words of more
than one syllable cross my lips without hooting and
hollering in a *most* unladylike manner.

I got calls and e-mails from people I don't know,
asking for help with their poetry or telling me about
their rocky childhoods, since my rocky childhood
was part of the article. A fellow teacher left a nice
note in my mailbox and a rubber stamp with four
cats on it, in honor of my cats, who were mentioned
in the paper by name.

Meanwhile, I have been running one of my
Poetry Boot Camps, a workshop I do on the internet
that requires enormous concentration and long
hours. So I haven't been free to bask in any glory
because there just hasn't been time. This is *very*
good for my character. Heaven forbid I should
sashay around town hoping people will notice me
and say "Oh, there goes that famous poet."

Even the phrase "famous poet" is ridiculous,
since probably only one person in 50 has read
a poem this year and even some of my students
can't name our National Poet Laureate. You could
be Walt Whitman and still walk down the street
unrecognized.

But in fact, I do want to be famous, and I want
to be famous exactly like this: so my bank manager
will come up and hug me; so women I see only in the
early mornings in our least-flattering clothes will
feel free to tease me. I am not aiming for limousines,
champagne, or flash bulbs. I think they would make
me deeply miserable. I want a direct connection
to other people — and the sense of belonging that
comes with being known. Because of that rocky
childhood, I've often felt alienated, outside the
windows looking in, and what I want more than
anything is to be included.

Which brings me to the subject of pledge drives. That may seem like a *non-sequitur*, but it ain't. This radio station you're listening to is one of the first ways I felt included in my town. Driving back from a trip, the signal would finally come in, and even 50 miles away, I knew I was home.

For about a year I just enjoyed listening to the station. Then someone's voice during a pledge drive got to me. I hated to think that some day her particular grace and goofiness might go off the air. So I called from a Shell station outside Fairfield, just at the end of her show, and pledged 20 bucks. Try it! It works like a charm. Once you're part of KVMR, trust me, you don't need a limousine. You belong.

Zanzibar

Last week a friend invited me to a pot-luck
dinner party based on recipes from Zanzibar. After
I promised to bring tropical-fruit salad and got
off the phone, I raced into the bathroom to find
Zanzibar. I knew it was part of Africa, but was it a
country, a city, an island, a region? Was Zanzibar a
colonial name for somewhere that now had a more
politically-correct title?

I scanned the shower curtain. I think Babar
and Celeste, beloved elephants from the French
children's stories, came from Zanzibar. I found
Madagascar, and Ghana, Botswana, Rwanda, and
South Africa. I reminded myself where Iraq and Iran
are, so I don't become one of those stupid Americans
who can't find them on a map, but there was no sign
of Zanzibar that far north. I paused to be amazed
all over again at how far above the U.S. Europe is —
San Francisco and Washington D.C. are on the same

latitude as Madrid. I looked at Tanzania and Kenya
while a Paul Simon tune ran through my head, from
the album he did with Ladysmith Black Mambazo.

Running into the bathroom is not really an adult
response to questions of geography, but I've just never
been very adult. For the last 20 years I've had a map-
of-the-world shower curtain. I've had six of them.
Some wear out: you know how they break through
around the holes and you patch the tear with a little
duct tape but then they rip again? And some become
so politically outdated they're worse than useless.
I got the latest so I could see Latvia, Estonia, and
Lithuania's outlines again, not just the huge pink
kitchen sink of the Soviet Union. My aunt Vija comes
from Latvia, and I have a proprietary interest.

The shower curtain is perfect for big-picture
questions: where's Svalbard in relation to
Spitzbergen? Where the heck is the Caspian Sea?
Or, if I'm reading Patrick O'Brian's Aubrey/Maturin
novels about Napoleonic naval battles, I can find
Brest, Gibraltar, and Mahon.

But Zanzibar was hiding. I sat down on the closed
toilet lid and searched Africa inch by inch. *Nada*.
Alright, on to Plan B. I plucked my Webster's Pocket
Atlas of the World from a bookshelf in the living room,
and finally tracked it down on page 133. Not just one

island, Zanzibar's an archipelago on the south-east
coast of Africa, above Madagascar, and is the top
worldwide producer of cloves. It united with Tangan-
yik-a to form the country of Tanzan-*i*-a in 1964 — I
was nine. And it's only about the size of Detroit, so it
would never show up on a shower curtain.

Having located Zanzibar, I could go to the dinner
with a clear conscience. We ate coconut rice, chicken
kabobs, deep-fried lentil balls, and two tropical
fruit salads. Mine had papaya, mango, lime, and
blueberries. Blueberries are not *strictly* tropical,
coming primarily from Maine, but I couldn't help it.
They looked so good, and I like to bend the rules at
least a little bit whenever possible.

Ghosts

Where I live, in the Sierra foothills, this is the most magical time of year. Spring comes to us like a rising tide, up from the flowering almond orchards on the valley floor, through blossoming plum trees and vivid mustard to the cheerful daffodils sprinkled in front yards and along highways. The plum trees break open first; willow fronds turn neon yellow. Then the pears bloom, the magnolias, and a week later the apples and crabapples start. At this time of year the fruit trees flowering in out-of-the-way places show you where old homesteads used to be. I always think of the ghosts of people who lived here before us: miners, laborers newly come from China or County Clare, the shadows of the Maidu and their forebears. I think of native women beating their washing on the Yuba's granite rocks and those tough pioneers stooped over cast iron kettles stirring whatever someone had managed to shoot and skin.

I think of my own ghosts, too, at this time of
year — especially my mother. This was the month
it became clear the chemo wasn't working, that her
system was too worn down for alternative efforts.
She flew back from a clinic in Arizona to live her
last weeks at home, with her children around her.
Her sister and brother-in-law flew out from Boston
and stayed a whole month, saving our sanity. We all
dosey-doed around each other like square dancers
who couldn't quite hear the caller but were doing
their best not to trample each others' toes.

My mother had an old Japanese plum tree
outside her bedroom window, underplanted with
foxgloves. In the intermittent fog and sun of early
spring, that tree put on the show of its life. Mom,
even when she could keep down nothing more than
popsicles and morphine, would look out the window
from her hospital bed and whisper "plums!"

It's not an accident that my heart rolls over
when I see a flowering tree, or that my sister
can tell you what little brown anonymous bird is
scratching in the dust. We grew up watching our
mother appreciate the world's beauty. It was part
of her nature — something so essential we picked
it up without noticing. Our brothers have it, too.
It's both a kind of reverence and a bargain with

the world. As if my mother was able to take beauty in twice: first whole, as "what God hath wrought," and then piecemeal, item by item. I can almost hear her saying under her breath, eyeing a tide pool or a stand of pampas grass backlit by sunset: "OK, if you're going to make something this gorgeous, I'm going to remember it." I think, in a fairly difficult life, beauty kept her going.

When I was a kid and we went shopping for fabric, my mother always turned the material over to see the wrong side. She did this with leaves, too, on walks in the woods. She told me that sometimes, unintentionally, the back was lovelier than the front.

It was kind of a secret between us.

The Gleaning

Last Saturday I went back to the organic farm where I get most of my vegetables for an end-of-the-year "gleaning." Half the reason I went was in honor of this old-fashioned, long-forgotten word, which comes from the Gaelic and means to gather anything little by little, especially what's left after the regular gatherers are finished. The other half of the reason was because I'm a big fan of sharing.

From the earliest sibling hand-to-hand combat through kindergarten's mottos and grammar school recess foursquare games, most Americans have been encouraged to share, take turns, and let Tom, Dick, or Harriet go next. This isn't always a lesson that sticks, as you can see just by looking at the current administration. As we grow up, "share and share alike" seems to get muscled aside by "it's a dog-eat-dog world," and "every man for himself." This might be the human animal's natural state, entwined in our DNA, or a function of watching sports on TV, where a winning-at-all-costs mentality prevails. I don't know — it's just so disappointing. So whenever there's a chance to promote or participate in sharing, I take it.

When I got to the farm — which is five open acres sloped at a lovely angle — it was filled with busy gleaners, from the septuagenarian hauling hot pepper plants out by the roots to a trio of little girls dropping cherry tomatoes carefully into their pockets. Men, women, and turquoise-haired teenagers were twisting eggplants, squashes, and seven kinds of tomatoes from their vines. They filled cardboard boxes, grocery bags, and every type of basket. People toted watermelons and baseball-bat zucchinis down the zinnia-lined promenade between the fields to their cars.

The farmers devised the gleaning as a way to strengthen bonds with the community, as well as not waste end-of-season produce that would otherwise be plowed under when they sowed their winter cover crop. These leftovers were perfectly tasty, despite not being farm-stand-perfect in size or ripeness. Since early June the farmers have been picking produce, so there was a certain slap-happiness in their demeanor as they stood aside

and watched a hundred people swarming the rows,
fending for themselves among the tomatillos,
carrots, and bolted basil.

There was a donation box, but we could take
what we wanted, and were urged to take no more
than we could use. The Interfaith Food Ministry
hauled off ten huge boxes. A man I spoke to was
going to make fried green tomatoes because of the
movie title. I was thinking of ratatouille but it was
impossible to get any picking done since I stopped
to talk to so many friends. I came away, finally,
with three eggplants, two green peppers, and a bag
of tomatoes someone handed me, delighted at the
beautiful fall day, the bustling scene, and the spirit
of generosity. I put ten bucks in the kitty.

On the way home, I found myself humming:
"And in the end, the love you take… is equal to the
love you make."

Flint & Kent

One of my grandfathers was the manager of a department store in Buffalo, NY called Flint & Kent. This was a store like City of Paris or I. Magnin's in San Francisco used to be, before department stores branched out and diluted themselves, before you could find a Nordstrom's in every shopping mall with the right zip code in America. Since he died when I was seven, what I know about him comes from stories my dad told me.

My grandfather used to give lectures about retailing at business schools on the East Coast, and was famous for the way he talked about a retailer's year. *First*, he would say, *you pay your rent. That's where all your earnings go until late May. Then you pay your sales staff, your administrators, your utility bills. By this time it's the end of July. All of August covers your advertising, and in early September you begin to pay for the whole year's inventory.* Then he would pause and smile at his students. *At 4 p.m. on Christmas Eve, you have paid off your expenses for the entire year. From 4 to 10, or whenever you decide to close the shop, that's your profit.*

I love this story because of how it deflates the idea of making easy money. Instead of thinking about selling a fur coat, say, at the usual keystone mark-up (which means double) for $2000 and imagining you can make a clear thousand on it, he put the selling of that fur coat into its proper context, alongside the rent on the 4 square feet of display space it would take up, the proportion of salespeople's paychecks, how much the ads cost, the heat, the air conditioning, what tiny part of the salary of the guy at the white baby grand on the mezzanine this fur coat would have to carry.

After I got out of college and had knocked around for a couple of years, I worked in retail for a small store in Cambridge, selling and managing and later buying. I used to look out at Brattle St. on snowy December afternoons and think about my grandfather's story, imagining the bright lights of Flint & Kent, the store lit up like an ocean liner moored in downtown Buffalo. I thought of the bustle and rush as Christmas got closer, my grandfather walking through the aisles, noticing things, tweaking a hanger here and there, making jokes with his staff, drinking a little eggnog with the piano player.

And in many holiday seasons since, even though I try hard to make things instead of buying them, I have found myself out in the fray on Christmas Eve afternoon, as though a bell had rung inside my head. It's a crazy time to try to shop. People are out of their minds. But I want to be part of the throng, to feel that urgency of humanity: gaiety mingled with panic under the colored lights.

And I can see my grandfather's smile. It's 4 p.m. Everything from here on out is profit.

YIELD

Poetry Reading at Point Arena

This week I drove four hours to a little town on the coast to do a poetry reading. I hadn't given a reading in eight months, and I've been struggling with my writing, so this was kind of a test.

I arrived early enough to take a hike along some bluffs and then watch the sun set from the end of a fishing pier, while drinking a gin-free gin & tonic. I thought about having the gin, but I haven't been drinking for almost 15 years now, and I knew it would make me unpredictable — probably in the direction of sappy and overly confiding, but maybe the other way, toward sarcastic and arrogant, or possibly just swinging wildly in a charming manner between the two.

After my tonic & lime, and no green flash from the setting sun, I walked back to the car. I passed a truck with a huge black dog leaning out the camper window, front feet and all. I stopped and said hello,

and after a long pause he started barking so loudly
I flinched and stepped back. His owner clambered
out of the cab to reprimand the dog, whose name
turned out to be Little Neptune, and who gave me
a thorough wrist bath while Fritz, the owner, was
welcoming me to Point Arena, telling me how sorry
he was to have to miss my reading, and asking if I
were married.

I'm not married. I'm not in love. I'm not
dating anyone at the moment, and although once
in a while I'm ferociously lonely, that didn't seem
useful information to give this friendly 70-year-old
whose breath smelled ever so slightly of gin — even
though he was handsome and the part of my brain
that wears a leather jacket and too much eyeliner
remarked that if I were to kiss him, together we
could create the flavor of a whole gin & tonic.

Instead, I smiled and lied: "Yes, I am, but
thank you," and he bowed. The dog, meanwhile,
was working his enormous tongue in circles up my
forearm, which didn't feel half-bad, so I thought it
might be time to go.

The reading was wonderful. An accomplished
open mike, good acoustics. An audience of about
20, who listened carefully. My new poems sounded
reasonably good together. Afterward, I was paid

$100, which just about covered my gas, and escorted
on an enthusiastic late night tour of Point Arena, a
town that's only two blocks long.

Why am I telling you this story? I guess because
it's so moving to me in this sometimes cold world
to be reminded that strangers can come together so
effortlessly. I'm always amazed when people show
up to hear poems by someone they've never met
about a river they've never seen. And it was good to
be reminded that resistance on my part to this kind
of connection — whether by way of gin, sarcasm,
loneliness, even erotic daydreams about large black
dogs — is worth fending off. It betrays something
fundamental and human that deserves not to be
betrayed.

Visualize Using Your Turn Signal

Now that the political bumper stickers of the last year are beside the point, my eye keeps being drawn to one about world peace. Actually, it's not about world peace, it expressly says "Never Mind World Peace: Visualize Using Your Turn Signal."

Well, this is right up my alley. I am famously short-tempered to begin with, and driving behind some nitwit who veers left unexpectedly, not to mention those delightful people who turn at intersections you're trying to cross — nearly smacking your front bumper with their unlit red plastic signal covers — causes long strings of inventive profanity in several languages to unspool off my tongue.

When I was a kid in California, driving behavior was legendarily civilized. Children were safe in crosswalks from Mexico to Oregon, and people whose turn signal bulbs had burned out opened their windows even in the rain to use their hands.

My relatives in Massachusetts talked about this
with awe.

Unfortunately, those courtesies have gone the
way of the triceratops. Most drivers are still able to
make themselves wait their turn at four-way stops
in my rural county, but in cities...forget about it.
You take your life in your hands today crossing any
California street.

The funny thing is, I think this has everything
to do with world peace. I think world peace could be
achieved by more people using their turn signals.
Think about it: what are signals for? They're a
way to communicate with your fellow drivers, to
say "This is where I'm going," and "Look out, I'm
turning left here," or "Slow down, don't get hurt,
I'm changing lanes." What is this, if not concern for
each other, the very bedrock of world peace?

And the converse, of course, is also true: when
you don't signal, the message rings clearly: "I am
alone on the road," or "This street is mine, too
bad for you," or "It's not my fault you hit that tree
because you couldn't tell I was turning." Not using
your turn signal is base self-absorption — a denial of
community in the most immediate way.

Before we go any further, let me assure you
that I too sometimes forget to signal — we all have

occasional lapses or get distracted, and nobody's perfect. But when you've let yourself really get out of the habit altogether, it's worth considering why, and maybe putting yourself into a personal turn signal re-training boot camp. Try it! Signal even though you're in a left- or right-turn-only lane. Signal when no other cars or pedestrians are in sight. Signal at rotaries, why not? It's all good practice.

Then the next time you're zipping along in the fast lane and suddenly remember you're supposed to take this exit, you'll automatically flick that little lever and not terrify everyone around you by unexpectedly lurching across three lanes. In 30 years, children all over the world — a kinder, more peaceful world — will thank you.

The Loss of Nameless Things

A couple of years ago, a documentary film
was made about my friend and ex-fiancé Tad. His
real name is Oakley Maxwell Hall, III. Tad was a
young hotshot playwright and ran a little theater
company in upstate New York in the late '70s. One
night he mysteriously fell off a bridge onto his
head, rearranging much of his frontal lobe, to the
devastation of his family and friends. I'm not sure
that he was devastated, because his devastation-
tracking mechanism got smashed in the fall. But he
was certainly changed.

The documentary was prompted by one of
Tad's plays — written before the accident — being
produced here in Nevada City, 25 years later. The
play describes the last days of explorer Merriwether
Lewis and his mysterious death — was it murder?
accident? suicide? I think the parallels were too
great for the filmmaker to resist, and then when he

did some exploratory filming and realized how much the camera loved Tad's face, he was hooked. This was all a huge big deal for Tad, who had not been the center of attention for a very long time and was suddenly seeing his play staged and starring in a film about himself.

The play got wonderful reviews and had its six-week run. The film turned out to be interesting and moving and even those of us who know Tad well learned something new from it. It's been on the festival circuit for two years or so, winning prizes and creating a small stir. Some of us worried what it would be like for Tad when the original hubbub died down — if he would be crushed — but he has remained on his brain-injury-induced even keel the whole time, anchored by his daily practice of writing.

I spend a lot of my time telling people that writing can save them. It's a way to get problems and traumas out of your body and onto the page, where you have more control over them. It can boost your immune system in scientifically measurable ways. And, as in Tad's case, writing can be a dedication, the scaffolding from which to reassemble a shattered mind.

Seven days a week Tad gets up at 5:00 in the morning and writes. I don't always understand what he's writing, or approve of his subject matter — once he had all our cats (with pseudonyms of course) engaging in pornographic romps with aliens — but I'm so impressed that he does it! Over the long years since his fall, writing has helped him hold onto, and maybe reinvent, his essential self.

Now another hubbub is underway. Last week the documentary began to air around the country on Public Television. The official website had 89,000 hits the first night it played. Things aren't quite that crazy for Tad, but he's been getting e-mails from old friends, directors asking for his play, and people with brain injuries who want to talk to him.

The film's title is a haunting phrase Tad wrote himself: *The Loss of Nameless Things*. I love the way that sounds, and how it ties together the aftermath of his fall and Merriwether Lewis's last days. It's very artful. But sometimes I think it's not quite accurate.

What Tad lost seems all too concrete, to me. It's what he gained that's mysterious and unnamable.

Family

In my e-mail program, there's a list of categories on the left side where I can file messages I want to keep. The first is "Editors." The second is "Family." Family includes my three siblings and 15 cousins, two of my aunts, one niece, two sisters-in-law, my mom's best friend Lois, and my favorite ex-boyfriend Tad Hall. It also includes Tad's parents, sisters, nephews, niece, and two of his other ex-girlfriends.

Tad died three years ago of a heart attack. He was 60, smoked unfiltered Camel cigarettes with great enthusiasm, and his internal organs had been rearranged by a dreadful fall when he was 29 that smashed his brain and changed his life. He wasn't fond of vegetables. None of these things are necessarily causal, but they might be contributing factors to his death.

He had been walking toward or away from a back porch in Albany, N.Y. The coroner said he was likely dead before he hit the floor. Even if coroners are paid to tell us things like this by way of comfort, I'm not sure Tad would have minded lying on the floor for a little while, even if he was in some pain. His pain threshold was high, and he was perennially curious. I can imagine him admiring the unaccustomed view of chair legs and baseboards and thinking, like the writer he was, "Oh, *this* is what it's like!"

I met Tad at a writer's conference. In the 12 years that I saw him daily, he got up between four and five in the morning and wrote for several hours every day. When we lived together, he had a tiny red writing studio in the back yard. Later he used a converted chicken coop behind his parents' garage. Before his accident, he had been a hotshot playwright running a theater company in upstate New York. I think writing every day, even when his subject was aliens named after our cats, helped his brain on its long road of repair and gave him the focus he needed to organize his life.

Tad and I lived together for five years, and then, dear listener, despite his incredible kindness, I didn't marry him. I bought a wreck of a house across town and he spent eight months helping me make it livable. Sometimes his help was valuable, and sometimes, as when he primed and painted a bathroom and then primed it again, there were glitches. Once I moved in, he phoned me at 9:00 every morning for the next seven years and we saw each other daily. He's the only boyfriend I ever left who came with me. He helped me stack wood and I taught him, over and over, to open a new document on his computer so he could start the next novel. Our terms of endearment varied, but I usually called him "Lulu," and he called me "Little Horrible." He took a lot of naps on my bed. He helped me bury four cats.

Three years ago he moved back to upstate New York, the site of his professional triumphs and his terrible fall, to live with a new girlfriend, someone he'd known when he was running Lexington Conservatory Theater in the 1970s. I still sent him my shoes after two or three years of wear had made them wide enough for his feet. About once a week I got an e-mail in response to radio essays I sent him. I always asked his permission before I read anything about him in public, and he always had the same response. I can hear it in my head right now as I silently inquire about this one. "Molly," he'd say, in his gruff bass voice, inhaling the smoke from a Camel straight.

"What you write is about you, it's not about me."

Naked Lady Pear Sauce

Fifteen years ago, when I was making the
house I live in habitable — when I bought it there
was ivy growing out of the bathtub spigot — I
cannily put in a window wherever I might have
reason to stand up and do any work. I believe if
you can look outside while working, your day will
be a lot more cheerful. Many of the windows were
from salvage yards. There are two over the kitchen
sink and a long narrow one turned on its side in
the bathroom, so I can look down at the yard while
I'm brushing my teeth. Every room has at least
one window and some have as many as nine. From
the kitchen I can watch daffodils bloom, roses
change color, and Jupiter's Beard try to take over
the known universe. Out the bathroom window
I see a little ruffle of wisteria trained on a trellis
attached to the house, a few branches of silver
maple, and one 30-foot-tall pear tree.

For some reason, my brain thinks pears are French. Do you grapple with fruit-geography rules in your head? My brain has very strong opinions. Bananas are Cuban, grapes are, of course, Italian, olives are Spanish, and pears are French. Apples are as American as apple pie, of necessity to make the cliché work. Most stone fruit — peaches, plums, nectarines — are international, but cherries are unequivocally British and apricots belong to Turkey. I'm not going to argue if you think this is ridiculous: it is ridiculous. I just haven't been able to stop.

Having a pear tree is a wonderful thing. In the odd years, it doesn't produce much: maybe 25 pears. But the even years, whoooo-eeee! I currently have almost 50 lbs. of pears in my kitchen, ripening on all the counter tops. Some are rock-hard green, some are kind of rubbery, and a few are starting to move from ripe yellow into rotten so I'd better deal with them today. I've given away at least another 50 lbs. to people who dropped by with fruit ladders and bushel baskets. The top third of the tree, I can see from the bathroom, is still laden with pears, but birds are beginning to poke holes in them, and the distance they have to fall makes them less than ideal for saving.

Until I moved to this house, I didn't know what
to do with a plethora of pears, but last fall some
friends and I decided if you could make applesauce
then you could certainly make pearsauce, and we
spent a weekend in a steaming kitchen proving this.
I'm a fan of pears poached in red wine, so we added
some zinfandel to the mixture and boiled the liquor
off, and of course, everything tastes better with
cardamom. The product turned out a lovely kind of
fleshy color, and it was so hot in that kitchen we had
to take our shirts off, which, along with the French
influence, is how it has come to be known far and
wide as Naked Lady Pear Sauce...

The, Ahem, Monologues

The other day a friend of mine, while talking
on the radio about political columnist Molly Ivins
having died, by mistake said "Molly Fisk" instead.
This caused a small ruckus: people called in to see
if it was true, and someone even stopped by the
station. Nobody phoned me, alas, so I wasn't able
to use Mark Twain's great line: "The rumors of my
death have been greatly exaggerated!" I *will* get a
Mark Twain fix this week, however, because he once
stood on the stage of the Nevada Theater, our local
landmark, and next Wednesday night I'll be up there
myself, with six other women, reading *The Vagina
Monologues*.

Even after a month of rehearsals, I can barely
say the title. That word — the one that isn't
Monologues — just does not trip blithely off my
tongue. Who invented it, anyway? The image in my
head is of 12th century academics gathered around a

table examining two cadavers, male and female, and calling out suggestions: *ulna! femur! kidney! vagina!*

Good *grief*.

In one of the Monologues, the word is likened to a medical instrument: *Quick, Nurse! Hand me the vagina!* It does have an icy, utilitarian sound to it, as opposed to some of its nicknames, which I will not mention here, although about 400 of them are used in the performance.

I volunteered to be in this cast precisely because the word made me so uncomfortable. The first time I saw the reading, as a 48-year-old who considered herself both unflappable and a feminist, I nearly crawled out of my skin because they said *vagina* 37 times in the first ten minutes. After blushing and squirming in my seat, I got mad. Adult women should be able to rattle off the names of their body parts without flinching! But how would we learn to do so when there's no precedent for it? The word rarely appears in novels. No sitcom actors say *vagina*, no film stars — it doesn't exist in advertising. People can barely say *tampon*, much less *vagina*.

This, of course, is Eve Ensler's point: to break the taboo. She's done a good job: ten years after writing *The Vagina Monologues* — using material gleaned from interviews with 200 women — it will be staged 3000 times this month, around the world, to benefit groups that help women in trouble.

If Molly Ivins were still alive, she'd remind us this is how change occurs: somebody gets a bee in her bonnet and doesn't rest until thousands of people are paying attention. It's what she did herself, and like Ensler, she made her revelations really funny. Because Molly's gone, all of us have to step into her shoes. Women need to tell the truth about what they know. Even if the words are hard to say. *Especially* if the words are hard to say.

I've always liked Mark Twain's irreverence. On stage Wednesday night, I'll give his ghost a wink. But then, in honor of Molly Ivins, and thanks to Eve Ensler, I'm going to open my mouth.

Over and over and over again, I'm going to say *VAGINA*.

Bread & Roses

I don't know what's come over me lately but
I cry at the drop of a hat. Yesterday it was an old
labor song whose lyrics I was trying to remember, so
I looked them up on-line. It was May Day, and my
town is physically erupting in flowers, plus everyone
was posting flowers on Facebook, and May Poles,
and stories about Beltane and the pagan origins
of the day. I love colorful ribbons twined around a
pole by dancing children as much as anyone, but I
wanted to remind myself of the day's history as a
focus of protest in America, too.

So there I am, looking up May Day on that
famous search engine whose name I refuse to use as
a verb, and there are the song lyrics, plain against
a white background, no java script, no graphics, no
old photographs, and I read the first verse and burst
into tears.

As we go marching, marching, in the beauty of the day,
A million darkened kitchens, a thousand mill lofts gray,
Are touched with all the radiance that a sudden sun discloses,
For the people hear us singing: Bread and Roses! Bread and Roses!

I'm crying for so many reasons. I miss Utah
Phillips, and what an anchor of conviction he was about
fighting for fairness in the world and people having
enough to eat. He lived in this town, and I'll tell you, it
was a great thing to have him here, anarchist, activist,
folk-singer, reminding us what matters.

I'm crying for all the women, past and present,
who are treated so badly. Some with violence and
death, including some of our labor foremothers, and
some with just the modern-day veneer of dismissal,
as when Secretary of State Clinton got asked who
made the clothes she wore, a question no one will
ever ask John Kerry, her successor.

As we go marching, marching, we battle too for men,
For they are women's children, and we mother them again.
Our lives shall not be sweated from birth until life closes;
Hearts starve as well as bodies; give us bread, but give us roses.

I'm crying with gratitude for the women and
men whose protesting brought us the five-day work

week, child labor laws, and eight-hour days. No one I know does much marching any more, and I don't understand why. I'm crying because it feels as though people don't remember how to band together to fight unfairness and I hate to see our great-grandparents' efforts wasted.

Maybe, too, I'm crying because I feel so helpless to do anything about any of it. It's a beautiful day again today, warm and sunny, flowers blooming like crazy all over town. Life seems so good.

As we go marching, marching, we bring the greater days,
The rising of the women means the rising of the race.
No more the drudge and idler, ten that toil where one reposes,
But a sharing of life's glories: Bread and roses, bread and roses.

Being Fat

This week I gave my students an exercise they hate: to write about what they really *don't* want to write about. And since I wanted to support them, and because it's so good for a writer to be challenge herself, I decided I'd better do the exercise, too.

What I really don't want to write about is being fat. Specifically, that I weigh more than Arnold Schwarzenegger. Somehow, being a heroin addict or an alcoholic in this culture has a certain cachet, while being fat is just, well, gross. Think Keith Richards and Bonnie Raitt (both now in recovery, thank god) versus, say, late Elvis, Marlon Brando, Orson Welles. Or Kate Winslet gaining 20 lbs. to the horror of her publicist, and you'll see what I mean. Fat is ranked at the bottom of our culture's — pardon me — food chain, below wife-beaters, child molesters, and axe murderers. It's insane.

In addition to condoned national disgust,
and putting my name in the same sentence with
Arnold Schwarzenegger's, here's what else I
dislike about being fat: the unexpectedly snug
fit of airline seats; having to completely relearn
my balance on cross country skis, ice skates, and
bicycles; and the way I look.

But being fat has taught me a lot that I'm glad
to know. First of all, paradoxically and conveniently,
becoming larger has made me invisible, particularly
to construction workers, whose whistles and
disgusting remarks plagued me a lot in my 20's and
30's. I've learned to be more deeply compassionate
toward anyone else on the margins of our narrow-
minded society, like people of color, gays and
lesbians, the homeless, the chronically ill and
mentally ill, the poor, Vietnam Vets, and anyone who
doesn't speak English very well.

It's also boosted my political thinking
enormously. Once you're outside the culture's
target market, you can see more clearly how that
massive advertising machine really works. I'm not
suggesting that a few Oreos for breakfast constitute
political action — you are, after all, still supporting
a brand — but to reject the carefully choreographed
steps expected of American women in the way of

beauty and standard sexiness is a great relief as well as a liberation. And it's good to discover that standard sexiness is not the only kind there is.

But the best part is that when you're fat, and the cultural norms of beauty leave you out, you are free to embrace a different sort of beauty, one that's lasting and nourishing and that we get to define for ourselves, based on infinite variety. One we bring forth whole and shimmering out of our open, elegant minds, and our generous hearts.

Act Like a Post

I've just been invited to go to a ground-breaking ceremony in Trinidad. Not Trinidad, California — the island of Trinidad, in the country of Trinidad & Tobago, down at the bottom of the Caribbean near Venezuela. You're wondering what I could possibly have done to get an invitation like this, aren't you? The short answer is that I learned how to act like a post.

My grandmother, Jonnie Fisk, was a backyard birdwatcher who parlayed her hobby into a calling at the age of 50. She got a banding license and for years drove from her home in Massachusetts down the Eastern Seaboard to Miami, banding birds on the barrier beaches along the way. After a month or two in Florida, running the southernmost banding station in the country, she turned around and drove back again. According to a *New York Times* article I just found on the Internet, "she worked harder and longer studying one small bird, the Least tern, and spent more time and money trying to protect the species than anyone in the world."

When I was a kid, I spent a lot of time with her on Cape Cod. She was the Cape's "Tern Warden," which meant that she studied the birds' migrations, their population, and their feeding habits and did her best to keep dune buggies off their nesting sites. Many mornings we'd go out to some lonely stretch of sand and my grandmother would sit down near a nesting site and tell me to act like a post. There were many posts nearby, bearing signs to warn dune buggies that the area was off-limits.

After some minutes of stillness, we'd see a tern chick moving. It was my job to keep my eye on it while she stood up and walked over to pick it up and band it. The chicks were so well-camouflaged they almost melted into the sand. When I lost one, we both had to stay absolutely motionless until it moved again. Meanwhile, all this time the adult terns would be whirling overhead and dive-bombing us, trying to attack our heads with their razor-sharp bills, which was why we wore hats.

Along with defending terns, my grandmother made bird inventories of land newly donated to the Nature Conservancy and helped to found a couple of nature centers. One's in New Jersey, and the other is, you guessed it, on the island of Trinidad. Sometime in November, I'll get on a plane and fly to Port au Prince with my Aunt Amanda, to be present for the groundbreaking ceremony for a new building named in my grandmother's honor.

I think she would be pleased as punch and also highly embarrassed at this idea — she wasn't great at taking compliments, even though she liked them a lot. If she hadn't died 17 years ago and could come with us to see the first shovel of dirt lifted where someday will stand the Jonnie Fisk Administrative Complex, I'd tell her to take a deep breath, put on a big smile, and act like a post.

Birches

This morning around six a young birch tree I planted last fall snapped in half with such a resolute crack that it woke us all up. I sat bolt upright in bed and the cats did too, riveted in the direction of the window, ears cocked. The sound was hard to figure out. I thought maybe a Canada goose had landed on the roof.

There was no noise but the rain. Sid leapt off the bed and onto the windowsill, followed by Angus, Red Jack, and Gracie, and I finally got up and looked out, seeing immediately that the birch had fallen because it's right next to the one that broke last week which I hadn't dug out yet and carted away.

I pay attention to sound. My mother and her father both began to go deaf in their forties. Grandpa wore hearing aids and looked thoughtful when you asked him a question, as though he were carefully considering the answer. Then he'd say

something totally off the point. Mom went through
20 years of innovation in hearing aids before she
learned American Sign. Chemo knocked the last
sounds from her ears, but she could read lips pretty
well by then, especially those of her children. I've
tried this in restaurants and watching foreign
movies and I can't do it at all, it's incredibly hard.

My siblings and I are constantly making jokes
about deafness because we're terrified it will
happen to us, too — a day doesn't go by when
I don't notice some kind of sound: rain on the
roof, birdsong, my engine idling at a stop sign, a
weekend chain saw. So when the birch snapped
and woke me up, one of the 200 simultaneous
swirling thoughts in my head, right after "Am I
alive?" was, "Hey! I can still hear!"

I planted those two birches as memorials to my
mother and my great-aunt Net, who died within a
year of each other. They'd both spent a lot of time in
Vermont and loved the white bark and whispering,
heart-shaped leaves. It's awful to plant trees in
memory of people you love and then have them
not thrive. It makes me feel like a bad daughter, as
though I didn't love them enough. No matter that
young trees are known to break like this when sap
rises too fast.

When my mother called to tell me she had
cancer, there was a TTY operator on the line with us
who typed my responses so they appeared on a little
screen on Mom's phone and she could read them.
It was a pretty tough conversation, as you might
imagine, and the operator kept having to type in
"sound of crying."

I hope I never lose my hearing, but in case I do,
I've been collecting every noise I want to remember.
Including Mozart and wind chimes and the ocean
during a storm. Including cats purring in my arms.
Including that operator's "I'm so sorry," after my
mother hung up. And the crack of a tree breaking
in the early morning, and the swish of branches
brushing down the side of a house as they fall.

ONE WAY

Missing Coffee Cup

Well, it's been one of those days. I just spent
half an hour looking for my coffee cup, which had
disappeared off the face of the earth. I'm one of
those people with a strong visual sense: I notice
where objects are placed almost subliminally, and
can often tell you that your car keys are on the
mantel if I'm around when you've lost them. This
is a useful trait, although, naming no names, it's
been known to irritate those of my friends who had
something they were hoping I wouldn't notice.

The only problem is that when I lose stuff myself
it drives me instantaneously crazy. I knew I'd made
coffee at 6 a.m., and had sat on the sofa to drink
it, listening to the world wake up: trucks grinding
up 49 out of the river canyon, the early commuters
whizzing along Newtown Rd. Then the first birds; a
neighbor calling her dog. The stove finally beginning
to creak with the fire's heat.

I took a second cup (it's decaf) down to my
studio around 7:15, put it on the maple-leaf shaped
coaster next to my mousepad, and got so involved
returning miscellaneous e-mails that I forgot to
drink it. That was the first place I looked just
now. Then my bureau, where I might have put it
while I was getting dressed, the kitchen counters,
back to the table next to the sofa. It was not in the
bathroom, not by my bed. I checked the rusty stool
outside the front door where I put things down
when I come in from the car. I even went up to the
laundry room, though it couldn't possibly be there.

By this time the Mulder half of my brain (you
know, from the X-Files) is wondering, in a purely
academic way, what space aliens would do with my
yellow ceramic coffee cup, while the Scully side,
rejecting space aliens out of hand, is considering
whether my brother might really drive the three
hours from Marin to indulge his passion for practical
jokes. Because clearly the cup is gone, and clearly I
didn't lose it. I'm actually surprised the sun is still
shining and gravity still works.

I check inside the icebox. Nope. I go sit outside
and try to forget about it. This doesn't work at
all, but it's warm and quiet and my mind does
calm down enough to notice a pair of nuthatches

scoping out one of my birdhouses. Each one in turn goes in through the little round hole and then pokes its head out and looks at the other. Nuthatches are very good birds. They're the only ones that can walk straight downhill on a tree, and I've always liked them.

I walk back inside to heat up some soup for lunch, and open the microwave. I'm not going crazy after all. There it is. One nearly full coffee cup, patiently waiting for me to find it, invisible all this time behind a white plastic appliance door.

I'm quite relieved. Not least to know that space aliens haven't yet found Newtown Rd. And you probably thought a poet's life was boring!

Lipstick

This morning I grabbed a pair of shoes to step into the driveway for the newspaper, not caring whether they matched my nightgown. As I came down the path, paper in hand, I recognized the sound my shoes were making on the cement — it was my mother, dressed to go out, clicking across the wooden floor in heels. Before the image of me in a nightgown and heels gets a foothold in your brain, though, let me say that I had thrown on a pair of flats. I'm just breaking them in and the sharp edge of the flat heel makes a click identical to the one I heard in 1963.

If you're a man, maybe you sat on the edge of the tub to watch your dad shave, wondering what it felt like to be a grown up. If you're a woman, you might have thought this as you watched your mom put on her lipstick. I loved the careful application, one eye on the mirror, the pressing of lips together

to even out the color, blotting them by kissing a
Kleenex, and then the sight of that red or pink half-
open mouth glimpsed as it floated from my mother's
hand into the waste basket.

Mom wore lipstick and perfume but like her
mother and sister, no eye shadow or mascara.
Since that side of the family were Unitarians
and I was a little girl who could put two and two
together, I deduced that Unitarians didn't believe
in eye makeup. It made sense that there couldn't
be a Holy Trinity of cosmetics if you only believed
in one God, and lipstick seemed to have won out.
My theory was reinforced later by the televangelist
Tammy Faye Bakker, whose mascara looked like
she had tarantulas on her eyelids — clear proof
that she believed in all sorts of odd things. By then
I was trying to keep lipstick on my own lips. This
is harder than it looks. It smears off onto nearby
objects — my teeth, the rims of glasses, the tines
of salad forks. And forget about kissing! Even a
peck on the cheek leaves half of it stuck to the
kissee's face — you can't make out in the stuff
without access to damp paper towels. This was my
first lesson in the duplicity of glamour: we wear
lipstick to look sexy, but it impedes the simplest
move in that direction.

After my mother blotted her lips and tossed the Kleenex, she clicked down the long curving stairway to meet my father at the front door, calling out last-minute instructions to the babysitter. That's where this memory ends. We might have played Chutes & Ladders or Crazy Eights after dinner. We were almost always asleep when our parents got home.

The next morning it was back to Wheatina and carpools, our mom in a dirndl skirt she'd made herself and a Norwegian sweater, no lipstick in sight. Instead of *Ma Griffe*, she smelled of those quintessential Unitarian scents: Yardley's English Lavender and melted butter.

Happily Ever After

Today is the first sunny day around here in
about 200 years. I should be dancing around in the
yard, reveling in sunlight. I should be walking down
Broad St. greeting shopkeepers with my famously
brilliant smile, having a wonderful time just being
alive. Is that what I'm doing? No. Instead, I've been
thinking all morning about the fact that I'm not
married. And while some people might consider this
with relief or even glee, in me it brings about an
Eeyore-esque moroseness.

It's not that I've never been in love — I'm regular-
ly falling in love, and I've co-habited with boyfriends
much of my life. It's not that none of them asked me
to marry him — I turned two proposals down. And
it's not that I think marriage is all that fabulous an
institution, since, growing up in the 20th century, I
recognize the constraints it's put on many women's
lives. And then, of course, there's the divorce rate.

But not ever having been married makes me feel like a social outcast. As though I weren't American, or womanly or something. It pushes a very old button about being absolutely and totally unlovable.

My friend Jane has said more than once that I should just go to Reno and marry my favorite and most-recent ex-boyfriend and then divorce him and get all this over with. I love it when she tells me this, because it's such a ludicrous idea that it cheers me up. And the ex-boyfriend would probably be glad to oblige. But I don't think it would solve the problem. I have no idea what would solve the problem, other than falling in love and marrying somebody, which doesn't seem to be in the cards this week.

I have an embarrassing suspicion that there's magical thinking involved too, like the idea that if I'm not married, I won't get to live happily ever after. None of those fairy tales ever said that the maiden aunt got to live happily ever after. Usually she was eaten by a wolf. I think the movie business bears some responsibility for the fantasy, too. Seeing Tom Hanks and Meg Ryan holding hands and gazing at a sunset as the credits roll makes happily-ever-after seem more real. It's not real at all, of course. They're playing characters who are only 26 and have been lovers for approximately two weeks. Anyone sitting next to you in the theater can predict a few pitfalls in their future.

I'm not even sure that happily-ever-after would be that great. I think it might get boring. Not that I'm wishing Meg and Tom ill, of course, I just think 60 years of "yes, darling" could drive a person nuts. When was the last time you were happy for more than a couple of days in a row, anyway? What about the other feelings a marriage might provoke, like joy, annoyance, passion, rage, sadness, delight, and annoyance? Isn't the variety what makes life interesting?

In order to live happily ever after, I think you may need a lobotomy. But don't ask me, I've never been married.

Great Big Life-Threatening
Kitty-Cats R Us

Last week a friend and I went out for lunch.
Although not the same age, we're both "of a certain
age," as the French like to say, meaning not young,
and possibly getting close to the top of the hill, but
not over it. People came up to say hello, and one, a
man of a certain age, wrote my friend later to say
we'd looked like "a couple of panthers."

At first I was puzzled — the mountains where we
live are not habitat for panthers. Did he mean Black
Panthers, even though both of us are white? That
made no sense. Then the light dawned — ohhhhh!
Not panthers, but "cougars!" Whether this was a joke
or the result of a failing memory, I don't know.

"Cougar," is a mostly-21st century name for
older women who date younger men, the implication
being that no sane man would do this of his own
volition, so predation, stealth, and trickery on

the part of the woman must have been involved.
Charming idea, isn't it? I have some feelings about
this, not least because older men have been going
out with younger women since the invention of dirt
and never coined a derisive name for themselves.
Suddenly when the tables are turned, women get a
snarky label.

I asked what people thought of this at my
favorite coffee shop. One woman, in her 30's, feels
age and maturity are so far apart the numbers
really don't matter, and therefore "cougar" wasn't a
concept she gave any time to. A woman in her 50's
disliked the word, but felt she might not have any
right to complain since she was in the other camp:
20 years her husband's junior.

The only man I spoke to about this couldn't
stop laughing at the panther mistake, and we didn't
get an intelligible response. Another customer
grinned and said "I'm a wildlife biologist! You're
not going to get anything out of me but admiration
for real cougars, so I think it's a fine name for older
women." I asked what she'd call older men who date
younger women, and she said she'd probably start
with "creep," and "slime ball."

I've been using "hyena," myself. Leaving out
true love, where age doesn't matter, the usual

trade has been older men's power, influence, and wealth in exchange for younger women's beauty, energy, and youth.

When I broached this subject at a dinner party of people over 50, I got gales of laughter, and one prescient wag said, "You can feel irritated at the word cougar, but don't forget we're really too old for it. The demographic they're talking about is 45-year-old women and 30-year-old men. They don't even realize the rest of us are still alive!"

Cougar does irritate me, and there's really only one thing I can think to do about it.

From now on, dear readers, you have permission to call me a panther.

Divine Spark

This week, after nine years of nomadic nights
and fund-raising, our local homeless shelter finally
broke ground on its new, permanent building.
Actually, the President of the Board just planted a
maple tree in a redwood half-barrel, ceremoniously,
but "breaking ground" is what they call it. Now
remodeling can begin, changing this former church-
and-office-building into a 54-bed shelter with
kitchen, showers, laundry, and meeting rooms for
guests as well as offices for the staff. The shelter
is named Utah's Place, after folksinger U. Utah
Phillips, who helped start it.

Also this week, another local champion of our
homeless population, someone who has been feeding
people hot and cold meals here for many years using
the name Divine Spark, died in a car crash on his
way back from delivering food to the Pine Ridge
Indian Reservation in South Dakota. The irony of

seven days being packed equally with happiness and sadness, and so closely revolving around the homeless, did not go unnoticed in our town.

Last night I sat on the sofa and watched the full moon rise. It comes up over my driveway at this time of year, huge and white between two little oaks. I wasn't thinking about homelessness, I was thinking about age. How I'd worked with an 80-year-old client that morning, and then had dinner with a 32-year-old friend. That I'd see my oldest student the next day, who's 95, and am slated to give driving lessons to a 15-year-old I adore. I was thinking, sort of distractedly while counting crochet stitches, how much I treasure everyone I know and how encircled I feel by people of all ages — somehow, at 57, in the right place. I don't usually sit around thinking things like this, and it suddenly turned into something large and profound. I felt more and more quiet and amazed, grateful, lucky, the moon lifting into the sky, my heart full of love.

When I heard Tomas had died on the road, one of my thoughts was, "That could so easily be me." I'm always off in a car alone, heading for Mt. Lassen, or southern Utah. That's what it would be like if I hit black ice and went off a cliff: people finding out over a couple of days and telling each

other, shocked, disbelieving. Probably I will leave
about the same-sized hole in this town that Tomas
did. But I also felt a wild jolt of gladness that I'm
not dead yet. It wasn't me this time.

Gratitude and grace spread all through me and
out into the living room. I'm glad I have a home, with
heat and light and running water. I'm glad I went
to the ceremony at Utah's Place, even though I was
horribly late. I'm grateful for eyes to see the moon,
and that I took the time to find out this one's name,
even though it's kind of gross: it's the Worm Moon.

I'm so glad the last time I saw Tomas on the
sidewalk, I smiled at him and he smiled back.

The Speed of the Sound of Loneliness

One big drawback to living with cats is they're
not good at holding a conversation. Monologues, yes,
which I mostly understand, that have to do with
food, competition, my lap, and bad weather. And
food. I would actually be interested to hear if blue
jays taste better than gophers and why they don't
eat that one internal organ always left on the carpet.
I bet they could tell me what's happened to some
of our cats who've disappeared. But about these
subjects they are mum.

I have lively discussions with the baristas at
my favorite coffee shop, and my friends and I talk
each others' ears off. But I actually spend most
of my days either by myself or teaching, which is
another monologue sport. Facebook provides an
interesting social scene I never expected, and now
and then a good conversation emerges, but mostly it
tends toward one-liners or argumentation. Writing

has aspects of conversation to it — I get to propose
something I'm interested in. But no one responds,
or they respond a few days later, after they've heard
me on the radio.

What I'm thinking about right now is the paper-
thin line between solitude and loneliness — why
the first is replenishing and the second debilitating,
when in both cases you might just be sitting on your
front stoop listening to wind in the trees. A mother
of three teenagers would call it blessed solitude
when her kids are all at the movies and she gets a
minute to herself. Whereas a bachelor could feel
crushed by loneliness sitting out there wondering
what the hell to make for dinner for the two-
hundredth time.

I call it solitude when I'm in a good mood and
saw a lot of people the day before. But if it's the fifth
night by myself and the phone is silent, I'm near
the screaming level of loneliness. The quickest fix
for me is to go to the grocery store. Seeing all those
checkers I've known for years is oddly comforting,
and reminds me I live in this particular town
and haven't just drifted off the edge of the world.
Usually then I can gather up enough energy to call a
friend or make some kind of plan so I won't be alone
the next day.

People in families have no idea what privileges they enjoy: to be touched, to belong, to engage in conversation. I don't mean to idealize anything... we all know families can be hard, too. But the dilemma of managing your own loneliness is often solved just by proximity. People who live in isolation have to be on the ball not to let it get out of hand. That cliff-edge over the Sea of Despond is always closer than you think.

Which is one reason I frequent my favorite coffee shop almost every morning. Today, as I was writing, a friend settled into his chair beside me and said,

"For my 16th birthday my dad took me bear hunting."

Now that's what I call a conversation-starter.

This Is My Life?

Even though I'm old enough to be your mother, sometimes I still look around and think, "Is this really my life?!?" How did I end up this far from the ocean? How on earth did I never have children? Where's that husband I was going to share the ups and downs with? I've never even gotten divorced, for Pete's sake, which is practically unAmerican...

Maybe some people step back when they're my age and say: THERE, I did it! I discovered this virus or passed these laws. I built that skyscraper, or even that chicken coop. I raised five kids and now look how great they are! What happens to me is I get floored by minutiae. Squishing toothpaste onto my brush, I suddenly think, "Again? I have to do this AGAIN?!" Washing dishes, I look at a blue glass I bought in Cambridge in 1983 and do the math. "I've been washing this glass for 29 years?! Are you KIDDING me????"

When I was young, I thought growing older involved some sort of transcendence. Acquiring experience would confer wisdom, and then everything would change. I didn't analyze this, clearly, if I thought toothpaste would no longer be required, but it seems to have quietly become a pillar of my world view.

I do feel wise, sometimes. When I overhear young people wrestling with a problem that seems extraordinarily small, I recognize how different I am now than when I was 30. When a friend chooses one more lunatic lover and says the same thing she said about the last one, I don't try to stop her any more. I know now she's on her own path. But the transcendent part never happened. Lots of things have changed in my life, of course. Phones are no longer attached to the wall, and I can't do a jack-knife dive any more. But the big shift I was expecting has never occurred, the one where I finally figure everything out and begin living my real life.

Neuroscientists and psychologists agree that human beings spend almost every waking hour making meaning out of their circumstances. We have little control over what happens to us, but a lot over the story we tell about it. And any story we tell is just that, a story. Good or bad, they're equally unverifiable. Since we have a choice, why not make the story positive, one that pleases us or has a little hope in it, rather than one laced with disappointment?

I think of this, washing that glass again. Yes, actually, this IS my life. I'm surrounded by friends. I turned out to be good at writing poetry. I live 150 miles from the nearest ocean, but half a mile from a great swimming hole. I still have quite a few teeth in my head that need brushing.

And, I have managed not to break a blue drinking glass from Crate & Barrel during 29 years of continuous use! I call that lucky.

Yellow Bird

Once upon a time I was 32, and lived half a block from the center of Harvard Square in a pale blue triple-decker with Rastafarian-colored balusters under its railings. My friend Sally owned the house and lived on the top floor, and I lived on the bottom. In the middle were a rotating cast of characters who shall remain nameless because I can't recall their names.

Sally was my parents' age, as well as a friend of theirs, but she and I became pals and did many things together, including stand around in Harvard Square listening to a wonderful steel drum band that used to play there. In summer, with our windows open, we could hear it from the house, and would call each other up and say "They're here!" just the way people in my current neighborhood call each other when we hear Sandhill cranes overhead on their twice-a-year

migrations. We'd squinch on our flip-flops and
run around the corner to gather with the crowd,
swaying, singing along, and dancing.

At some point, Sal and I started throwing big
parties at this shared house, and she had the great
idea to hire the band. So for about five years we
had a tradition of steel-drum music in the driveway,
a couple of grills putting out jerk chicken, with
both our apartments wide open and people milling
around late into the night. A good deal of beer and
rum were consumed, and Lord knows what else.
Spliffs, I am sure, at the very least.

If you haven't heard steel drum music before,
it's a cheerful, bell-like sound often accompanying
Harry Belafonte and others whose music derives
from the West Indies. We called it "pan," which is
what the band called it, in their lilting Trinidadian
voices. This band had five players and seven drums,
and though I never got close enough to see inside
the curved bowl where they thumped their mallets,
the resonant optimism of those notes still rings in
my ears.

Fast forward to a New Year's Day party here in
California and a motley but enthusiastic collection
of singers and guitars. I arrived just in time to
chime in on "Margaritaville," one of the sappiest

songs known to mankind. And lo, who should appear suddenly from a back bedroom, but a white guy with a steel drum to play an inspired solo!

While thanking my hostess at the end of the night, I mentioned the drum.

"Oh, he gives lessons," she told me, "And they're free!"

"I'm taking them," I heard myself say.

"Oh you are, are you?" I asked myself later in the car. "You've got time for one more thing?"

"Yes!" I replied. "Not for everything. But if it's light-hearted, and free, and makes me grin in spite of myself, I have time for that."

Which is why, for about ten minutes last Thursday evening, you could hear me playing "Yellow Bird" on the tenor steel drum, all by myself...

Give Peace a Chance

The first anti-war protest I went to was in
Berkeley in 1970. I was 15. All I remember is that
the crowd was humongous. We walked in a circle
and sang "All we are saying is Give Peace a Chance."
Despite the sense of elation from being in such a big
group, I got incredibly tired of that song.

I thought of this the other night as I stood on
the Broad St. bridge over Highway 49. There were
about a hundred people joined in a vigil against
President Bush's Iraq war, of which it was the
fourth anniversary. Most of the — hmmm — do
you call people holding a vigil "vigilantes?" Maybe
not. Most everyone was middle-aged except for a
few little kids. I overheard someone say he hadn't
expected to be doing this again in his sixties.

Bill was there, leaning against the railing in
dark glasses because his wounds from Viet Nam
have just begun, after decades of other pain,

wrecking his eyesight. Our local famous folksinger
Utah Phillips was there, whose tour of Korea left
him aimlessly riding the rails, trying to make sense
of his life. A guy who volunteered for Vista instead
of going to Nam stood next to a woman whose
husband flew helicopters over the Laotian jungle.
Each person there had some kind of story.

Look around and you'll see everything's
a story, from conversations overheard in the
check-out line to a kid's excuse for not doing his
homework. Think of what's issued forth from the
pulpit of any church! Humans live by stories. We
know each other through stories, we experience
our lives as a series of stories. Children want to
hear the same stories over and over, cementing all
kinds of information in their brains, helping them
to make sense of the world.

I stood on the bridge as the sky got darker,
watching the light from our candles brighten until it
was the only light, illuminating our faces, gleaming
from a distance like so many fireflies. Someone
started singing "All we are saying is Give Peace a
Chance," but luckily it didn't spread.

No one in Washington, D.C. gives a hoot that
we're doing this, I thought. Standing here for two
hours is not going to stop the war. But it's hugely

important to *us*, the ones who are here. It's an act
of humanity.

In holding this vigil we honored the people
who've died in Iraq: the 3,223 Americans and 60,000
Iraqis whose stories are over. We acknowledged their
bereft families. We stood in witness to the pain of
the survivors: the amputees and men and women
with shrapnel wounds and PTSD, whose stories the
war has irrevocably altered. We gathered on that
bridge representing an ancient human story, the one
that says life is valuable, not to be wasted.

We didn't need to sing that song over and over.
Our hundred candles flickering there in the dark
sang it for us.

Raised in Song

It turns out I am not a big fan of hysterical shopping. Nor of crowded roads, full parking lots, or the frayed nerves of my fellow humans. And I am *really* not a big fan of the American advertising machine, which I think has damaged the innate creativity of the average citizen almost beyond repair. So you can understand that I have mixed feelings about Christmas.

What cancels out all that other junk, for me, is the music. I love the way old-fashioned language comes so easily out of our mouths when we sing carols: "Hither page and stand by me, if thou knowst it telling," and "In thy dark streets shineth the everlasting light." When else in the 21st century would we use "thou" and "thy," or turn to someone and say "Hither," meaning: "Yo, dude! Get over here!" When we sing these songs we are joining our forebears, breathing at the same pauses, hitting the

same notes, holding those long vowels as they did at
A----men. We are embodying our connection to them,
which is a rare occasion in times that seem to be
wholly tuned to the modern and the very young.

The other thing I love about the music is the
sound of so many throats singing together. The
group, the community, raises its collective voice, and
it's thrilling. Everyone is welcome, no one is special,
and you don't have to be a professional to join in.
Singing carols, or Handel's Messiah at a sing-along,
is for us all — it's egalitarian. To be in the middle
of all that sound is incredibly powerful, and I think
healing — going straight to what in us needs to be
healed.

As someone whose vocation involves standing on
stage alone, and who very much *likes* that focused
attention and applause, singing in a group revives
me, reminds me that I'm part of something much,
much larger than myself. It's a good metaphor for
God or whatever we each believe in.

The words to the songs are part of the package,
too. Christmas carols are about joy: "Go tell it on
the mountain, over the hills and everywhere!" and
kindness: "Where meek souls will receive him still,
the dear Christ enters in." Whether you tend to
think, as I do, that the story of Christ is a teaching

tool rather than a memoir, it is still incredibly powerful to hear that story re-told, from all those different angles, in song.

This Christmas I'm avoiding parking lots and stores as much as possible, and going to every musical event I can find: concerts, carol parties, church carol services of every denomination. I'm singing Little Drummer Boy and The First Noel with my friends in the car while we tool around town at night, looking at Christmas lights. I hold in my mind that manger in Bethlehem, so long ago, beneath its unwavering star.

Even if we are not, all of us, faithful, we can still be joyful and triumphant.

U-TURNS

Today, Do Something Backward

Here's my advice: today, do something backward.
Wash your feet first in the shower instead of your
hair, or shave the *other* leg, the *other* cheek, start
reading a book at the end, get into your car on the
passenger side and crawl over the gear shift, walk
a different route, enter your office by the *back* door,
sleep with your feet on the pillow.

Whatever it is you always do, don't do it. Change
it just a tiny little bit. Go on, use a different bowl
for your cereal. Vacuum *before* you dust. Move your
desk so it's facing the other wall of your cubicle.

Someone did a study in the early '80s, thinking
that paint color on office walls could improve
productivity. And they were *amazed* at how well it
worked — changing the color from white to pale
green sent worker productivity up almost 25%. The
only trouble was, after a few months, peoples' output
sank to its original levels. Light green didn't seem to

have a long-term effect. So they repainted the walls a kind of beige-y brown and again, productivity soared. (You can see the punchline coming, right?) Three months later, everything's back the way it's always been. And then they got it — it's not the color of the walls that moves people to wake up and work harder, it's the *attention*.

So it is with us the rest of us. We repeat behavior because it's comforting and convenient and maybe saves time and then it starts to be the way we always do it, the way we prefer it, and it becomes habitual.

The trouble is, acting this way is like floating down a calm river in the sun, balancing your canoe paddle across the gunwales and humming a little nameless tune...just before you hear that funny rumbling sound, and your mind, in its lazy, somnolent state, adds two and two together to make "rapids." I'm not kidding, when you get attached to the way you always do things, you are in big trouble. The universe arranges disasters for people like you.

Of course, doing something backward takes too much time and is hopelessly contrived. But it's precisely the annoyance you feel about it that I'm trying to provoke. You're dying — all these habits, unjostled, will make your life so boring you won't

want to live it any more, and then you really *will*
buy the red sports car and leave your spouse for
someone who can't name all four Beatles.

What a shame that would be, not to mention a
huge cliché, and a load of grief that could so easily
have been avoided just by wearing unmatched socks
once in a while, mowing the lawn in figure eights,
eating lemon meringue pie for breakfast, and taking
an occasional overnight flight to Mallorca.

The Ladder of Success

Last summer I went hiking in southern Utah with a friend. The landscape was so incredible, and the food at the lodge where we stayed so delectable, that I organized a writing workshop for the same week this year, just so I could go back and visit this amazing place again.

I love being self-employed. Sure, I miss not having someone else pay my health insurance and retirement benefits, or contribute to a 401K, whatever that is... And I don't always relish being up at one in the morning designing yet another flyer to advertise my classes, or cleaning the living room on Sunday nights because I teach at home. But I love being free to invent sneaky ways to get what I want: like running a workshop in a beautiful out-of-the-way spot like Boulder, Utah.

Let's face it: I make, and have made on quite a few occasions, a rotten employee. I'm too pigheaded

and proud to work for other people with any grace. I
want to do things my way, and at my own pace. I'm
smart enough to be a pain in the neck questioning
management decisions, and not smart enough to
keep my own counsel. I'm rebellious at all times,
and for no real reason: it's a knee-jerk reaction to
stricture. And it's probably genetic: much of my
family is just as charmingly impossible as I am.

You should have seen me when I was a banker
in Chicago. I excuse my bad judgement in joining
an organization of 10,000 people in a conservative
profession, because my dad had just died and I
was too devastated to do anything but take the
best job I was offered and put my head down. By
the time I was ready to lift my head up, I was
working on the 10th floor of a 57-storey building in
downtown Chicago, running growth projections on
the Canadian timber industry. This was 1985, and I
was using very early computers, and doing a pretty
bad job of it. The 10th floor had 40 desks scattered
around one big room, and floor-to-ceiling windows
that didn't open. Maybe they knew there was a risk
of some of us getting so irate with the computers
that we would try to jump out the window. Finally
I realized that the only person in the whole bank
whose job I wanted was the woman who came

in to teach us to speak real English instead of "bankerese," and I quit.

I slid down the ladder of success in record-breaking time, ending up as a self-employed poetry teacher, perhaps the least lucrative of modern professions, and have been scrounging with great inventiveness ever since. No paid vacations? Just plan a workshop in your favorite location. It's not *exactly* a vacation, but it's pretty close, and besides, you're in total control.

Southern Utah in August is gorgeous, and the workshop could not have gone better — I'm definitely going back again next year.

But in the meantime, I'm looking into trans-Atlantic flights. Isn't Paris supposed to be fabulous in early May?

DDT

The first fight I ever remember hearing as a child was at the dinner table when my father's parents were visiting us in San Francisco. They were arguing about the presidential race between Richard Nixon and John F. Kennedy, my parents for Kennedy and my grandparents for Nixon. I have no idea what was said, I think I was six, but grown-ups yelling at the dinner table made a big impression on me. From then on, I understood that my grandmother was something intractable called a Republican. My grandfather died soon after, but I was close to my grandmother for the next 30 years. She showed me that it's possible to change your mind.

After my grandfather died, my grandmother started doing what she loved to do, which was watching birds. She already had a banding license and had been monitoring the birds she banded and sending the data to Fish & Game. She lived on

Cape Cod, but began driving her blue Volkswagen down the coast to Florida every autumn, netting and banding birds along the way, stopping in at wildlife reserves and Audubon stations and making friends.

When I was sent to visit her, she took me to walk the beaches, where it turned out she was tracking the use of DDT. I can't remember how DDT got into the ocean, but when seabirds eat fish with DDT in them, they hatch chicks who can't fly. My job was to look for feathers with very short shafts, and bring them to her, and then she'd send a big box of them to the scientists doing the study. When she found a malformed bird, which happened about once a week, she would send me up the beach ahead of her while she held it in her big hands, gently but tightly, so it couldn't draw breath, and later made a study-skin of it and sent it to the Laboratory of Ornithology at Cornell.

Somewhere on this journey, my grandmother's ideas about the world shifted. She learned about ecology from all her biologist friends. She met Rachel Carson. The DDT study really made her mad. She taught me to rinse plastic bags and dry them on the dishtowel rack instead of throwing them away when I was ten, and cooked out of *Diet for a Small Planet* before anyone I knew had even started to be vegetarian. The next time Nixon ran for president, she put a Eugene McCarthy sticker on her bumper.

I thought of her when I saw Al Gore's movie, *An Inconvenient Truth*. Al says that unless we change the way we live in the next three to five years, we'll be in irreversible trouble. The change he's talking about feels daunting to me, and I *already* eat organic food and turn off the water while I'm brushing my teeth.

The only thing that gives me a tiny bit of hope is remembering the way my grandmother changed. Even when overthrowing your most ingrained habits seems wildly unlikely, it's not impossible.

Too Small an Island

My sister Sarah just got back from Fiji and is sitting in my living room in her pajamas and a fading tan, reading e-mails. Two pairs of her shoes are on the floor over by the bookcase, and the cats have been having erotic moments rubbing their cheeks and ears all over them, especially the blue-green leather pumps. Her bag is on one chair, her laptop case in another, there's a pile of notebooks on the table, black pearl earrings gleam next to her toothbrush in the bathroom, and a cream-colored bra has ended up haphazardly across the arm of the love seat.

This is what Sarah is like — so alive that even her belongings explode out into the room, full of enthusiasm. When I sat down to write this essay and said "What do you think I should write about?" she told me a story about parrots.

Most parrots, as everyone knows, are brightly colored, their feathers intense hues of blue or

green or yellow, vivid almost to the point of neon.
But there's one, called the African Gray Parrot,
that's the opposite — a lovely shade of gray, just
as beautiful as the others, but nothing that would
shine in the dark, except it has a bright red tail.

When you go snorkeling, Sarah says, there are
millions of incredible fish, including parrot fish, in
all those same amazing parrot colors. And among
the parrot fish, there's a gray one, with a red tail!
"You can't think the universe lacks a sense of humor
when you come across something like this. What
other reason could there be?!?"

I love Sarah's wonder, her general readiness to be
delighted at the world. Even when her work, which
is of the professional consulting variety, takes her to
office buildings in Placerville, Edmonton, and Dallas
in the same week, she still manages to discover that
there's an elephant named Lucy in the Edmonton Zoo
that can paint pictures using her trunk, and to go and
meet her. No one else I know has so many adventures
or tells such good stories about them afterward.

Sarah and I are a year apart, and have not
always gotten along, to say the least. It's kind of a
miracle that we're even in the same living room.
The fact that we are is 50% attributable to me, and
50% attributable to her. We've worked hard on it.

She told me a story from Fiji which she says forms her new philosophy of life, and I think I might adopt it, too. A friend of hers watched two men — brothers or cousins — fighting in a bar, nearly killing each other. A couple of days later, this friend, who knew the two men, saw them talking amicably on the sidewalk. She turned away but one of them was walking in the same direction, and caught up to her. She told him how surprised she was to see them so friendly, she thought they hated each other.

"Oh, no," said the Fijian man. "It's too small an island for that."

Half a Squirrel

I really have no reason to complain. I'm in good health, and none of my family or friends is in desperate trouble. My mortgage got paid this month, my car is running well, and there's enough wood to last me through the rest of the winter. My life is actually fine, it only *feels* like I'm about to go stark raving mad.

For one thing, ants are invading the house and walking off with all the cat food. They've made a little black trail of themselves from the back door, along the kitchen wall behind my grandmother's old high-boy, down one short step, and then across the tile to the cat food bowl. They have somehow managed to lift pieces of dry cat food — which in human terms would be like me and all my friends getting together to raise a gas station off its foundations and take it home with us — and drag them back toward the door.

This is amazing, laudable, and revolting, all at the same time. But mostly what it is is expensive. I know this because every so often I've had to get an exterminator to spray the outside of the house. One trail of ants and some missing cat food I can handle, but it doesn't stop there. Unchecked, soon there will be ants crawling all over the ceiling, getting into the flour, the sugar, the yellow raisins — their writhing mass too horrible to contemplate.

And speaking of revolting, there's half a squirrel currently lying on the living room carpet. This used to be a whole squirrel, which, when the cat brought it in this morning, grossed me out so much I walked right out of the house and closed the door behind me, paced around in the driveway thinking that I just couldn't stand it any more, the way the cats are always bringing in gruesome things and there's no one here but me to cope. Bad enough to have to pick up cat barf that has little feet in it. Bad enough the sweet yellow and black feathers I keep finding under the bed, and the tidy piles of rodent intestines here and there.

I eventually went back inside where Gracie was crouching over her prize, picked up the squirrel by its beautiful gray tail, and threw it off the deck. I closed the doors and windows so she couldn't bring

it back in. But then, you know how it is — I went
about my day and it got sunny and I left the back
door open and now here's the squirrel's nether half:
tail, back legs and most of its torso with a gaping
wide red hole at the top, making me want to puke.
And I don't want to *know* what happened to the
front half. I hope it's at least the same squirrel.

Most of the time I love the world, but right
now I'm on Woody Allen's side: I am "at two" with
nature. How am I supposed to get any writing done
with battalions of ants crawling everywhere? It just
makes me itch. And what if the cats bring in some
godawful thing while I'm trying to teach poetry in
the living room?

I need help. At least tell me how to get bloodstains
off the carpet.

Dropping the Meat

A friend took me to dinner last week at a French restaurant. I'd never heard of the place, and it took us a minute to find it after we got lost in a maze of mini-mansions. Our waitress was maybe 30, and we also had a water-pourer who looked about 12 but could pour backwards out of his carafe with astonishing accuracy. There were some buspersons, too, and mid-meal an older woman came along to make sure we were happy. And we were: the food was delicious.

When the bill came, I asked if my friend had been a waitress. Had she ever, at Woolworth counters all over California. This is my question to gauge tip-size, when someone else is paying for my dinner. If you've waited tables, you know how much those tips matter. You're on your feet for hours, remembering orders, carrying heavy trays, remaining civil when people behave poorly. There's

a certain customer who feels free to treat you like
garbage just because you're waiting on them. Even
half a century later, you probably leave good-sized
tips yourself.

I once worked at Ferdinand's, in Cambridge,
Mass. — the kind of place you took your parents
after college graduation. We had to do this thing
I've never heard of since, maybe because the chef
was truly French. We had to figure out, after taking
an order, how long every cut of meat would take to
cook — and then calculate backwards so we could
walk into the kitchen and tell them when to begin
cooking it in order for everything to be done at the
same time. This was called "dropping the meat." So
if you had a table of 6, with 4 meat orders, you had
to zip into the kitchen four separate times and have
them start the pork chops, which took 8 minutes
(I'm making these times up), then the well-done
filet, which was 6, then the veal piccata, which was
5, then the rare filet, which was 4 and a half.

I have no idea how we did it: seven or eight
waiters in line in the kitchen and the cooks
ignoring us, but you had to have eye contact to
know they'd heard you, and meanwhile your meal
is getting screwed up because the line is so long. It
was a nightmare.

The ONLY thing that made this tolerable was the size of the tips. Waitpeople are legally paid far less than minimum wage because the government counts tips as part of their earnings. So when you don't get tipped well, it's hard to make a decent living. And if anything goes wrong in the kitchen — your eggs are poached hard instead of soft — there's no way a customer can take revenge except by reducing the tip, even though it wasn't your fault.

Waiters tip bussers out of their own tips, and sometimes a percentage to the kitchen staff, too. So even if you never once waited on a table, be generous: put down 20%. The food will taste better. And your harried waitressing brothers and sisters all over the world will thank you.

Uncle John

One of my uncles died yesterday. Uncle John. You've heard of him, his last name was Updike. Novelist, short story writer, poet, literary critic, art critic, essayist, husband, ex-husband, father, grandfather, and uncle. Fixture at *The New Yorker* from the age of 23. Winner of two Pulitzer Prizes and heaven knows what else. You don't always find his books in paperback at airport kiosks any more, but you sure used to.

Uncle John married my mother's older sister Mary in 1953. My mother married my dad the next year, and in due course four kids came along at about the same intervals to both couples, so we each had a cousin our own age. When we got together in the summer four harried adults and eight giddy children stuffed ourselves into John and Mary's Ford Falcon and drove to Crane's Beach to make sand castles. At the end of the day we stopped at the stand on Argilla Road for ice cream cones. If a child was done eating before the ice cream was gone, Irving, my dad, said: "Oh, just throw the cone out the window." And we did. They made a nice plop on the road.

It's very weird having someone famous in the family. Even though I've seen him at his most vividly human: throwing up when he had the flu, or snoring rather loudly as we cousins tiptoed past the sofa, it's hard not to feel the god-like aura that surrounds him in other people's minds. Some kid you're in college with or colleague at work breathes: "YOU are related to JOHN *UPDIKE*?!?!?" I usually admit that I am, but I never know what to do with my face — should I look pleased? Embarrassed? Repentant? My being his niece has nothing to do with anything. He was very present in my childhood, but more as part of a herd of grown-ups than as an individual who knew me well. In college I did some typing for him, before computers were invented. A decade later he commented — very diplomatically — on the first creative thing I ever wrote. He didn't encourage me to keep writing and he hasn't leant me a literary hand of any kind or asked to see my work. He did compliment my first CD of radio essays a few years ago, quite highly. It was such a shock to receive his note I forgot to thank him.

You can read about one of the summers we spent
on Martha's Vineyard in his short story, "The Day
the Rabbit Died." It was a real rabbit, and it really
died. Uncle John turned the eight of us kids into
four or five, mingling our characteristics. You can
read about throwing ice cream cones out the car
window in "Brother Grasshopper," which contains
every good family story about my dad. It also
contains a big lie. When it ran in *The New Yorker*
after Irving died, friends called to ask, worried, if
my father had *really* been a pornographic movie
producer. That hurt my feelings and made me
furious, but I loved Uncle John, in case it's starting
to sound like maybe I didn't. In the unconscious
way you love someone you know familially but not
personally: I'd recognize his foot on the stair, but
had no idea what he was thinking — he was just an
important part of the scenery.

I don't always like his writing, but how many
people get to have part of their own life preserved in
American fiction to look back on: those long summer
evenings playing volleyball and tennis, the adults
lapping up gin and tonics and flirting with each
other? And the kids, seemingly unaware, running
around on the lawn.

Slow Down

Yesterday I went to get my hair cut and colored. This two-hour event takes place in a small salon downtown that used to be a horse barn. When I'm sitting in the chair and Suzie is spritzing on some gooey concoction I don't know the name of, I think about those horses standing patiently as their coats were brushed and their tails were braided. We are not so different. The noise level would have been a little lower in the barn — no raucous music, fewer overlapping conversations. But I bet the pace was about the same.

When was the last time you sat for two hours and weren't watching TV or a movie? Not driving? Not on a plane? The world has been speeding up for a hundred years now: we rush around and accomplish things at a great rate — some things, anyway — and don't stop until we're asleep.

This is really bad for poetry. In order to write
poetry, you have to slow down. The subjects of
poems don't reveal themselves to a distracted eye
— a little stillness is required before our minds can
notice what's in front of us; before our hearts will
tell us how we feel and what we believe. The same is
true for reading poems. It's no accident that people
connect most deeply to the arts when they're in
some emotional turmoil. Turmoil slows down your
thinking, and then things like poetry can sneak in.

While Suzie is painting three different colors
onto my hair and wrapping each lock in tinfoil —
causing me to look like a stout, middle-aged-but-
soon-to-be-glamorous Martian — I can't put on my
glasses. I can't turn my head. I'm left alone with my
thoughts. I have time to squint at the joints on the
cabinet in front of me, or the colors on her swatch
card. I have time to wonder whether I'll ever learn
carpentry, or dye my hair completely green, and if
not, why not? Useful questions to consider, I think,
when you reach middle age.

So how do we slow down when we aren't at the
hair salon? It's easy, but it's radical. First, wherever
you go today, don't drive more than the speed limit.
This will be hard, because you're so accustomed
to rushing, but you can do it. You'll have to slow

down a little just to figure out what the speed limit actually is.

Second, get to wherever you're going five minutes early, and just sit. Don't flip through *National Geographic* or haul out your cell phone and text your Aunt Mabel. Sit still. Look out the window. What is the sky doing? Imagine you're a horse with a braided tail. You have instincts, but no obligations. Listen to your own breathing. See what happens. At the very least, your blood pressure will go down. You might even surprise yourself and think of a poem.

Which, after this annoying exercise is over, you can post on Facebook to show all your friends.

Ordinary Mastery

It's a foggy day in Fort Bragg, California but the rain has stopped. My hair is a damp halo around my head from the walk past Glass Beach, over the trestle, and into town. I'm drinking a cup of coffee at the local joint and if I close my eyes it sounds just like my own local joint back home: Neil Young from 1972 on the sound system, the clinking of cups and rustling of little white bakery bags as someone gets a latte for here and an oatmeal-apple scone to go. A couple of laptops are open, even though it's Sunday. Groups of older men — not much older than I am — are talking politics and the weather.

A friend and I have stolen three days on the coast. We wanted to smell the salt air and get out of our own lives, where the dust calls to be wiped from bookshelves and our work won't leave us alone. As you can see, though, I've brought a little of mine with me: this radio essay. Writing these is 90% fun and only 10% work, and they surely don't pay the rent, but still, I *am* a writer and this *is* writing, therefore some kind of work is involved.

Beneath my feminist 21st century exterior, I'm essentially an old-fashioned woman — I've got nostalgia and sentiment to spare. I came to this coffee shop today because this is where I wrote my first radio essay in October, 2004. I wanted to see what it felt like to write my 170th one here, too. 170!! Can you imagine? I'm not sure why, but our culture doesn't celebrate ordinary mastery. It notices the extremes — mastery like Joan Benoit winning the first women's Olympic marathon, or disaster like Bernie Madoff bilking thousands of people (and you could call this mastery of a sort). Cal Ripkin never missing a ballgame in 17 years got into the national news. But you and me quietly getting better and better at what we do — whether it's software design, museum exhibit dismantling, or writing down bits of your life to read on the radio — doesn't get much praise.

This is a crying shame. Ordinary people getting good at what they do makes the world go around. It brings a kind of satisfaction nothing else can, and millions of us are out here doing it. In complicated and simple ways, we're providing good examples for younger people, making our elders proud of us, and getting the job done. I'm probably never going to win the Pulitzer Prize in Poetry. But writing makes me happy, teaches me a lot, and helps other people now and then. It's worth doing. What are you better at now than you were when you started? Take a minute this week and make a list. Write down the ways in which what you do makes other people's lives better. Then give three cheers for yourself. It will feel idiotic, there at the kitchen table or in the front seat of your car. Other drivers will look at you funny. But do it anyway. Hip, hip, hooray for you and me and our good work.

Three big cheers for the huge contribution of the common human.

The Thing With Feathers

This weekend, someone I know is getting married. Someone else I know is due to have her second child. Last night a friend spent the night in the hospital after a mild heart attack. Eight people I know have cancer. One has shingles. Thirteen have the flu even though it's the middle of May. Three of the mothers of my oldest friends are very close to dying of old age, although one of them still likes to ride her exercise bike.

If you stand still for a minute in the center of your living room, the whole world will turn around you, as if you were the earth's axis. Every event you've ever heard of is happening simultaneously. All the opposites, the parallels, the coincidental amazements. Birth, death, lunch, and everything in between... Bugs are having sex, grizzly bears are fording rivers, eggs are breaking: some to reveal baby great blue herons, others to produce mushroom omelets at the Ritz.

A few of you may actually have stood still in
your living rooms when I suggested it, and some are
muttering at me under your breath, "Good grief,
Molly, this is nobody's news, get a grip."

I have a grip, thank you, but it's on very slippery
stuff: I think if you can feel the multiplicity of
everything happening, even just a little bit, then
you can find hope. And knowing how to find hope is
going to make your life better. Easier. Even if you're
75 and much of your life has already happened.
Even if you watch the nightly news.

Emily Dickinson starts her poem 314: "Hope
is the thing with feathers —/that perches in the
soul —/and sings the tune but not the words —/and
never stops — at all —"

It isn't just the hard things that are happening
all the time, it's the wonderful things, too.
Everywhere we look, the possibility exists for beauty,
kindness, love, compassion, literal and spiritual
flowering... I find this incredibly comforting.

Last night in the ER, watching my friend's blood
pressure recalibrate every 15 minutes and listening
to him grumble, I almost started to cry. He was so
unchanged, except for the ridiculous blue-flowered
nightgown on his over-six-foot frame. But then three
nurses came in, and a man who had nailed his hand

to a board by mistake, and someone needed water,
and I got distracted. My friend, a contractor, offered
to go home and get the right sort of hammer to
remove those nails, and everyone laughed.

Some day it'll be us in the coffin or compost
bin, but until then, we're alive, and anything could
happen. I probably won't get pregnant, but you
might. Maybe neither of us will kayak the width of
Lake Tahoe, but I'm going to breast stroke across
Scott's Flat Lake in August the way I did last year.
It's true, I might get shingles, or fall off a cliff. But
I could just as easily fall in love with someone from
Latvia and build a little house there whose roof was
composed of beautiful gray-green slate shingles.

You never know. Count on it.

Notes

The titles of three essays have been changed. In the
CD *Using Your Turn Signal Promotes World Peace*,
"Flint & Kent" was "My Grandfather's Theory of
Retailing;" "Birches" was "Losing Your Hearing;"
"Being Fat" was "Fat."

p. 15: "Watch Your Language," references the
bird-watching bibles: "Peterson:" *A Field Guide to
Western Birds* by Roger Tory Peterson, and "Sibley:"
The Sibley Guide to Birds by David Allen Sibley.

p. 71: The small store in Cambridge mentioned in
"Flint & Kent" is Clothware, now located at 1773
Mass. Ave, 02140 and still going strong.

p. 82: The PBS documentary about Tad's life,
The Loss of Nameless Things, is available from
Netflix and Hulu.com. More information at
thelossofnamelessthings.com. Tad's given name was
Oakley Maxwell Hall, III.

p. 100: The organization my grandmother helped
support is the Asa Wright Nature Center (asawright.

org), Spring Hill Estate, Arima, Trinidad & Tobago.
It's the place to go next time you need to see a Bat
Falcon, Green Kingfisher, Violaceous Euphonia or
even a Golden-headed Manakin.

p. 123: "The Speed of the Sound of Loneliness" is,
of course, the title of that wonderful song by John
Prine.

p. 164: "Ordinary Mastery" is dedicated to Robert
Lee Haycock.

p. 167: "The Thing With Feathers" is dedicated to
Bill Sheatsley.

Acknowledgements

I thanked so many people in my last book of essays that I don't know what to say here now. Let me just mention I'm insanely grateful for everyone's help and support and love. Public and private. Now and a long time ago. This means you, too, dear reader, dear listener, even if we're not Facebook friends. Yet.

Love to the ones who've known me the longest: Sarah and Peter and Sam. Mary & Bob. Amanda & Larry. Chan. Liz, Tete, David, Wambui, Michael, Miranda, and Donald. Bard, Laurel, Daniel, Rapp, David, Roger, and Raymond. Brad, Alice, and Doug. Tasha. Doris, Jinny & Joe, Ellen K., Ellen P., Sari, and Julie. Brian, Mike & Sue, Gary, and Carolyn. Margot & Fredot. Christal, Louise, Deborah P., Leah, and Teddi. Long-lost Deborah L., Rosemary. Lois. In memory of Jan, Margit, Sally, Taffy, Mummouse, Grandpa, Papa, and Uncle John.

The individual essays in this book originally aired as commentary on the News Hour of community radio station KVMR in Nevada City, CA or on KQED's California Report between 2004 and 2014 (© Molly Fisk). Download recent commentary for public radio airplay in a strict 4-minute format by contacting Creative PR at info@creativepr.org. There is no charge. This material is brought to you by the author and by KVMR 89.5 FM Nevada City, California through a grant from the Corporation for Public Broadcasting.

Selected essays in this book, some under different titles, appeared on womensvoicesforchange. com and barnowlvintage.com. Audio versions of 14 of the essays, read by the author, were collected on the limited-edition CD "Using Your Turn Signal Promotes World Peace."

About the Author

Molly Fisk is the author of *Blow-Drying a Chicken*, Observations from a Working Poet, the poetry collections, *The More Difficult Beauty, Listening to Winter, Terrain* (co-author) and *Salt Water Poems*, and two audio recordings of commentary, *Blow-Drying a Chicken* and *Using Your Turn Signal Promotes World Peace*.

Fisk has been awarded grants by the National Endowment for the Arts, the California Arts Council, and the Corporation for Public Broadcasting, and has been nominated for Poet Laureate of California. She's currently Poet Laureate of KVMR in Nevada City and Hell's Backbone Grill in Boulder, Utah. Fisk works as a life coach in the Skills for Change tradition and owns Poetry Boot Camp (poetrybootcamp.com). Visit her at mollyfisk.com.

To order signed and inscribed copies of
Using Your Turn Signal Promotes World Peace,
or any of Molly Fisk's other books, please visit
www.mollyfisk.com/writing.

CPSIA information can be obtained at www.ICGtesting.com
Printed in the USA
LVOW08s1412111015

457808LV00004B/232/P